IMAGES
of Rail

BLUE RIDGE
SCENIC RAILWAY

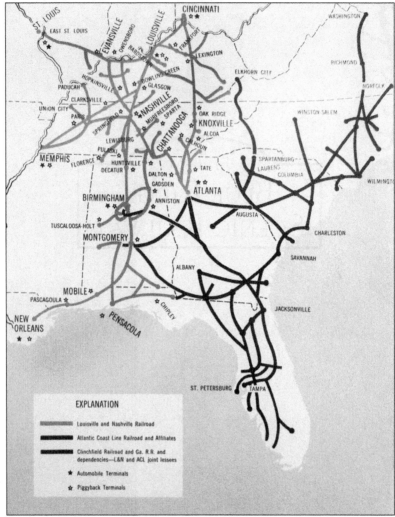

EXPLANATION

Louisville and Nashville Railroad

Atlantic Coast Line Railroad and Affiliates

Clinchfield Railroad and Ga. R.R. and
dependencies—L&N and ACL joint lessees

★ Automobile Terminals

☆ Piggyback Terminals

This mid-20th-century Louisville & Nashville (L&N) Railroad timetable system map shows the railroad extending outside of its general southeastern range. The Class I railroad provided service from St. Louis to New Orleans and Florida. At its height, L&N traveled more than 6,000 miles in its system and stretched into 13 states, with stops in major cities such as Louisville, Birmingham, Atlanta, Memphis, New Orleans, Mobile, Pensacola, St. Louis, Cincinnati, and Knoxville. The railroad began in 1850 and ended in 1982. (Courtesy of the City of Cartersville.)

ON THE COVER: This train crew standing in Blue Ridge in 1928 is complete, though unidentified, with an engineer, conductor, brakeman, and fireman. Each played an important role in the smooth operation of the train's system. The engineer's job was to operate the locomotive; the conductor was in charge of the entire train and the crew at large; the brakeman assisted the conductor, inspected the train, controlled the brakes, and assisted in switching; the fireman was part of the steam locomotive crew that fed the firebox with fuel. On a diesel train, the fireman would monitor the controls and assist the engineer. In his book *American Colossus: The Triumph of Capitalism, 1865–1900*, historian H.W. Brands says: "Railroads were the first industry to evolve a cadre of professional managers—men who specialized in railroad administration, developed standards for measuring performance, shared and debated new ideas, and published journals." (Courtesy of the Ducktown Basin Museum.)

IMAGES
of Rail

BLUE RIDGE
SCENIC RAILWAY

Melissa Beck

ARCADIA
PUBLISHING

Published by Arcadia Publishing
Charleston, South Carolina

Library of Congress Control Number: 2014943712

For all general information, please contact Arcadia Publishing:
Telephone 843-853-2070
Fax 843-853-0044
E-mail sales@arcadiapublishing.com
For customer service and orders:
Toll-Free 1-888-313-2665

Visit us on the Internet at www.arcadiapublishing.com

*To the people of Fannin and Polk Counties
for their fortitude throughout generations*

CONTENTS

ACKNOWLEDGMENTS

I would like to acknowledge the following individuals for their help in the creation of this book: Lynne Tipton, a graduate student in the American Studies program at Kennesaw State University, offered so much of her time, great energy, and research expertise; without her, libraries, archives, and various sleuthing methods would not have been nearly as much fun. Fannin history buffs Dale Dyer, Danny Mashburn, and Mike Queen generously shared photographs, remembrances, and reference books and often pointed me in the right direction. Samuel McMillan Freeman absorbed so many details of the work of his father, Samuel Jackson "Jack" Freeman, and shared them along with photographs, notes, and firsthand observations. Edye Daetwyler kindly went through her early Blue Ridge Scenic Railway photograph albums with me with the help of her grandson "Trainman" Andrew Lamanac, who has ridden the "Scenic" since he was three years old. I wish him well in the pursuit of his passion of becoming a locomotive engineer. Larry Dyer, lead trainman, and Tim Griffin, operations manager of Blue Ridge Scenic Railway, talked train history, donated scans of photographs, and allowed me to ride the wonderful Blue Ridge Scenic Railway so I could enjoy the full experience.

I learned many details about early Fannin and Polk Counties from two local history groups and appreciate their acceptance and willingness to share: the Copperhill Group for the Preservation of the Pictorial History of the Area and the Ducktown/Isabella/Postelle/Turtletown/Farner Picture Preservation Group. The following people were invaluable in lending me their ears and imparting their knowledge: Charles Castner, railroad collections consultant, the L&N Collection, University of Louisville; and Ken Rush, director, Ducktown Basin Museum. I am grateful to the librarians, archivists, curators, and volunteers for their help at these venues: Southern Museum of Civil War and Locomotive History, Marietta Museum of History, Cobb County Public Library System, Southeastern Railway Museum, Atlanta History Center, the National Archives at Atlanta, Bartow History Museum, History Branch and Archives of the Cleveland Bradley County Public Library, and Special Collections and Archives at the University of Louisville.

This book would not have been possible without the many individuals who so graciously sent me images from their personal collections—I hope I told your stories well. Arcadia Publishing's enthusiasm for this topic is also appreciated, and I thank my editor Liz Gurley for her guidance, patience, and hard work.

Finally, I thank my husband, Frank, and my son and daughter, Ben and Torie, for always being supportive and encouraging.

Image sources are identified by the following abbreviations:

BRSR: Blue Ridge Scenic Railway
CBCPL: History Branch and Archives of the Cleveland Bradley County Public Library
DBM: Ducktown Basin Museum
FCHF: Fannin County Heritage Foundation
L&N: Special Collections, University of Louisville, Louisville & Nashville Railroad Collection
LOC: The Library of Congress
McClung-UT: McClung Museum of Natural History & Culture, The University of Tennessee, Knoxville
PCHGS: Polk County Historical and Genealogical Society
TVA: Tennessee Valley Authority

INTRODUCTION

In the early part of the 19th century, the United States had noted Britain's successful railroad system and started to develop its own. By 1830, however, only 23 miles of track had been laid in this country. Railroads were in their infancy, yet the need for more rapid and dependable transportation excited government legislators and investors and inspired civil engineers and surveyors. In a relatively short time, these interested parties would combine to create a transportation system that would take off running.

The first railroads in Georgia appeared in the mid-1830s and ran out of Athens, Augusta, Macon, and Savannah, which was one of the most populated cities in the United States at the time. The Central Rail Road of Georgia (eventually reorganized as the Central of Georgia Railway) followed a route from Savannah to Macon, while the Georgia Railroad extended from Augusta to Athens. The Monroe Railroad (later the Macon & Augusta Railroad) started in Macon and traveled north to Forsyth.

In the northwestern area of the state, speculators had been considering a route toward the Tennessee River, the largest tributary of the Ohio River, where steamboats and barges were still the primary mode of transport. This goal led to the 1836 chartering of the state-owned Western & Atlantic (W&A) Railroad, which reached Chattanooga in 1851. The Western & Atlantic and Georgia Railroads converged in Atlanta at W&A's southern terminus, which had two large stations to accommodate the traffic. Atlanta's population growth—from 2,572 in 1850 to 21,789 in 1870—was commensurate with the rapid economic expansion created when rail systems become available.

By 1860, the South had several short lines serving certain towns and industries, but they did not interconnect like the railroad systems in the North and Midwest. This would prove to be a hindrance to the South during the Civil War, as they relied on trains to move supplies past enemy lines.

After the war, in the mid-1870s, Gen. William Phillips and J.B. Glover, both of whom had fought for the Confederacy, joined forces as proponents of forging northeast with the Marietta & North Georgia (M&NG) Railroad out of Marietta. Their goal was to link a war-torn, recuperating Atlanta with another growing trade hub—Knoxville. At the time, the W&A came from Atlanta as far up as Marietta and did not proceed east. Phillips and Glover raised the funds for their effort by selling stock in the M&NG, and with convict labor loaned to them by the state, they began building the railroad. However, they were thwarted by a rocky, pothole-filled right-of-way, and money ran short.

By 1882, they had reached Canton, Georgia—24 miles from Marietta. Then, the Kinsey brothers (Joseph and Abram) of Ohio, who owned interest in a copper mine near Murphy, North Carolina, offered to invest in extending the line to Murphy. The brothers had been hauling ore with oxen and wagons and were looking for a more expedient method of transportation. Soon, they had laid track in the vicinity of what would later become known as the Hook and Eye, a track near Tate Mountain between Talking Rock and Whitestone, Georgia, that had two sharp 45-degree angles (reverse curves).

The difficulty of laying track on the mountainous terrain pushed the Kinsey brothers to sell out to George R. Eager of Boston. Considered by some a wildcat speculator, Eager made a bet that he could get the railroad to Ellijay, Georgia, by November 30, 1883. He missed the deadline by one day, reportedly losing $10,000 in the bet. Still, he had already done better than most. Many enterprising railroad investors in the Reconstruction era petitioned for charters and, in some cases, even cleared land or laid track; however, most of them never made it past those initial stages.

In 1886, George Eager and his Marietta & North Georgia Railroad (M&NG) reached the town of Blue Ridge, which was 82 miles from Marietta. It had taken 10 years to build the track to this point in north Georgia, and they still needed to get to Knoxville over tough mountain terrain. Knoxville Southern expanded to the south, and M&NG expanded to the north, edging closer and closer to Bald Mountain. H.G. Monroe, a former brakeman, said, "This natural obstruction wasn't large as mountains go. But it had the shape of a streamliner's nose; its steep sides plunging headlong into the turbulent waters of the Hiwassee River. How to lower a train from these ledges to the canyon floor?" Indeed, in order to follow the Hiwassee River gorge as planned, they would have to drop several hundred feet down Bald Mountain in a few miles of track.

Eager's engineer, C.R. Walton, created a double switchback (also called a "W" because of its shape) on the southeast side of the mountain. The route was six miles of scary turns, plus a difficult switchback that only four cars could navigate at a time. When tracks can be built on flat, straight ground, trains use less energy, achieve better speeds, and accrue less wear and tear. Still, the M&NG forged on, and by 1890, 13 miles of track had been laid from Blue Ridge, Georgia, to the little Appalachian community of Copperhill, Tennessee. On June 30, 1890, 10 miles north of the state line at Copperhill, the Knoxville Southern line joined with Eager's M&NG. The next morning, the first train left from Georgia and traveled all the way to Knoxville.

Soon after, Eager took off with his cash; the railroad, having used its funds, went into receivership. J.B. Glover oversaw the sale of the railroad to pay off creditors, and after five years, the line became known as the Knoxville & Atlanta Railroad. Henry K. McHarg then purchased the line for $956,500 and changed its name to the Atlanta, Knoxville, & Northern Railway. McHarg deemed Blue Ridge its middle terminal. Next, McHarg had Louisville & Nashville Railroad (L&N) civil engineer T.A. Aber eliminate the dangerous double switchback by designing an 8,000-foot loop around the mountain that circles around it almost twice, ending in Farner, Tennessee. Then, Milton Smith, originally of New York, came down as part of L&N and purchased the railroad for $4 million—a tidy return on McHarg's investment. In 1906, L&N built the New Line to Cartersville, which was 28 miles shorter and on more navigable terrain. The Hiwassee Loop was used for freight, though, allowing Copperhill's mines to ship (on average) 1,000 cars of acid, crude copper, iron sinter, and ballast from the mines each month.

L&N now ran North Georgia's Old Line, the Hook and Eye, and the New Line—the more level and easy course from Etowah, Tennessee, to Cartersville, Georgia. Since 1890, L&N's lines had been open from Cincinnati south to New Orleans and west to St. Louis. L&N would go on to become one of the most successful railroads in history.

Investors and owners were happy to make financial gains, but for the people along the railroad's routes in north Georgia, the railroad offered more personal benefits. With the railroad came jobs, travel, population growth, and trade expansion. Family members worked for L&N. Locals lived near railroad employees, bought and sold products the trains freighted in and out, and could set their watches by the train's whistle.

Thomas Jefferson, who died in 1826, was said to have made the statement that it would take 1,000 years for the population to spread west of the Mississippi. Only 30 years after his death, 22,000 miles of railroad track traversed the United States; by 1890, that total had reached 164,000 miles. In the railroad's heyday, prior to 1920 and the rise of the automobile, 264,000 miles of track stretched across the United States—a very long way to come from a mere 23-mile beginning.

One

FORGING NEW TRAILS

North Georgia's first inhabitants were members of the Cherokee tribe. As settlers arrived, the Cherokee lived among the white men, trading with them and listening to their missionaries. When the New Echota Treaty went into effect in 1835, it displaced Indians to reservations, and the white settlers realized that the places where the Cherokee had once hunted, fished, and carved out footpaths were perfect lowland spots for future train tracks.

Interested parties had to first find ways to get railroads into the state's remote mountain region. Atlanta was the southernmost point of the railroad that would eventually extend north. The completion of this railroad became more of a priority for venture capitalists with their eyes on North Georgia after a man known only as Lemmons discovered gold just across the state line in Tennessee. This 1843 gold finding turned out to be insignificant compared with the copper he and later prospectors found. Removing the abundant copper ore from the mountains meant braving rugged, rocky trails. Loaded mule- or oxen-drawn wagons were slow and prone to toppling, and they took days to reach Dalton, which offered railroad access.

Western & Atlantic Railroad had already laid track from Atlanta to Marietta. In 1854, speculators received a charter to extend north. The Ellijay Railroad began but dissolved before laying any track. A Marietta, Canton & Ellijay railroad did not break ground, either. Other entrepreneurs made plans that also never came to fruition mainly due to funding or the upheaval caused by the Civil War.

The Marietta & North Georgia Railroad (M&NG) did find investors and began laying track north from Marietta in 1879, the same year it reached Canton. By 1884, M&NG tracks reached Ellijay, followed in short order by Blue Ridge, Mineral Bluff, and Culberson (by 1886). They reached Murphy in 1888, Ducktown in 1889, and—finally—the important trade location of Knoxville in 1890.

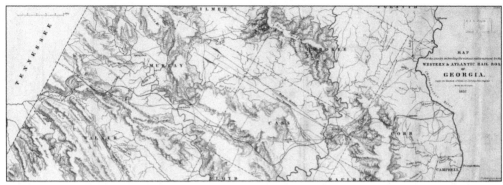

This "Map of the Country Embracing the Various Routes Surveyed for the Western and Atlantic Rail Road of Georgia, 1837," illustrates the routes charted by civil engineer and steam engine inventor Gen. Stephen Harriman Long, who had also scouted routes for the Baltimore & Ohio Railroad. Although the W&A tracks would be laid in DeKalb County (near the city of Atlanta) and head north toward Tennessee, the county to its east, marked "Harokee" [sic] on the map, was vast—over 6,000 square miles—and already under the control of the state government, which called it "Cherokee County." After the 1838 Indian Removal, the size of Cherokee County was greatly reduced. Work began in 1841 on the 138-mile route from Atlanta to Chattanooga, and after recessionary fits and starts, the W&A opened in 1850. (LOC.)

SE-QUO-YAH.

Around 1760, Sequoyah was born to a white trader and a Cherokee Indian in Monroe County, Tennessee. He is pictured here holding his creation, the Cherokee syllabary, a group of symbols used to represent his native language. (LOC.)

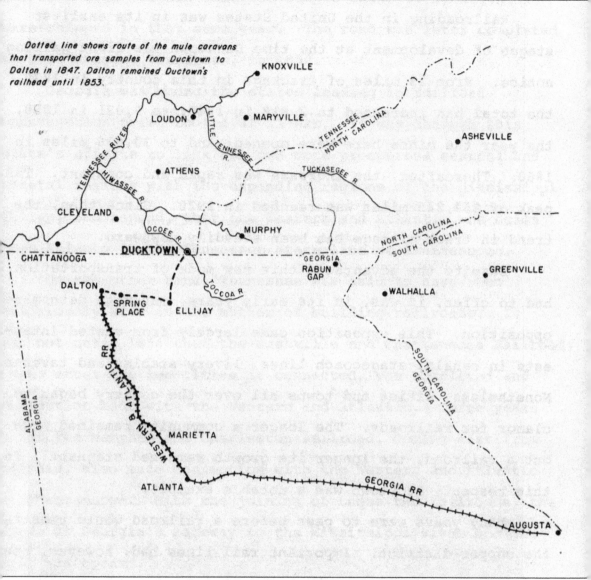

Dotted line shows route of the mule caravans that transported ore samples from Ducktown to Dalton in 1847. Dalton remained Ductown's railhead until 1853.

This hand-drawn map shows a wagon road from Ducktown to Dalton, a distance of approximately 60 miles. This was the first route used by miners for hauling ore to send it north via train (the Western & Atlantic Railroad out of Atlanta) for refinement. The trip involved days of grueling travel over rutted roads and nearly impassable mountains. In 1853, a much more navigable road built to Cleveland, Tennessee (approximately 35 miles from Ducktown), allowed miners to reach the East Tennessee & Georgia Railroad connector to Chattanooga and beyond. This image is included in Robert Edward Barclay's book *The Railroad Comes to Ducktown*. (PCHGS.)

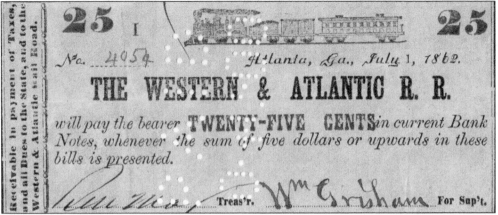

25 I

25

No. 4054

Atlanta, Ga., July 1, 1862.

THE WESTERN & ATLANTIC R. R.

will pay the bearer **TWENTY-FIVE CENTS** *in current Bank Notes, whenever the sum of five dollars or upwards in these bills is presented.*

Treas'r.

Wm Grisham For Sup't.

Prior to the adoption of a central banking system, state-chartered banks and other institutions issued their own money. The owners of railroads and bridges funded construction projects with bank notes that could be used as currency, as was the case with the Western & Atlantic Railroad (W&A). The W&A, which cost the State of Georgia nearly $5 million, was completed from Atlanta to Chattanooga by 1851. The state attempted to sell the railroad for $1 million in 1858, but there were no takers. (City of Cartersville.)

Georgia's railroad investors and planners established a trade route between Atlanta and Chattanooga, and the impact of that decision was made clear during the Civil War. In April 1862, James J. Andrews engineered the Great Locomotive Chase, during which Andrews and Union operatives stole a locomotive and slashed telegraph lines along the rails between the two major towns. The men were implementing Union general William Sherman's plan to isolate the South from supplies. Chattanooga (pictured around 1864) and Atlanta, along with Richmond, Virginia, were vitally important due to their railroads, as evidenced by the railways' involvement in the war. (LOC.)

After the Augusta-based Georgia Railroad reached Atlanta in 1845, the Atlanta Hotel opened. In 1846, the Macon & Western Railroad entered the picture, connecting from Macon and Savannah, and the Washington Hall hotel opened in Atlanta, which grew and soon had a mayor, a city council, a jail, wooden sidewalks, and a law forbidding business on Sunday. In 1851, the Western & Atlantic Railroad became the third railroad in Atlanta; this connected the city with Chattanooga and allowed for trade to the Midwest and points beyond. Atlanta's first union station (the large structure at right in the background) went up in 1853, and in 1854, the Atlanta & LaGrange Railroad joined the others. In 1855, the city had over 6,000 residents, and by 1860, 9,544 lived in the area. (LOC.)

This 1864 George N. Barnard glass-plate negative print of downtown Atlanta during Union occupation depicts a bustling area struck by wartime. In the foreground at left is Atlanta pioneer and businessman J.C. Hendrix's furniture company, a three-story brick building. The rounded top of the railroad roundhouse is visible in the background. Businessmen chat outside stores, soldiers roam the town, and horses and mules wait near conveyances. (LOC.)

In 1864, Union general William Sherman launched an attack on Atlanta, destroying train tracks, the railroad roundhouse, and many manufacturing plants. Here, his soldiers fire cannons directly at the rail yard and station. This image is attributed to photographer George N. Barnard. (LOC.)

Teamsters drove mules hauling wagonloads of ore along the Old Copper Road from Ducktown to Cleveland, Tennessee—a distance of 35 miles—for assaying. According to an early Knoxville newspaper, the *Journal & Tribune*, by June 1873, the Union Consolidated Mining Company had removed 8,476,873 pounds of ingot copper and employed 562 men running 16 furnaces. In 1873, Burra Burra Copper Company produced 917,329 pounds of ingot copper (valued at $192,630), employed 158 men, ran 9 furnaces that consumed 10,192 cords of wood, and paid $60,000 in wages. (CBCPL.)

Ducktown, Tennessee, was the first settlement in the Copper Basin, followed by Hawkinsville, Tennessee. When Harbert T. McCay bought land and settled in the Copper Basin area, he started a ferry business on the Toccoa/Ocoee River, and Hawkinsville became known as McCays. McCays eventually split into Copperhill on the Tennessee side, where the river is called the Ocoee, and McCaysville on the Georgia side, where the same river is called the Toccoa. (Ron Henry Collection.)

This 1884 map shows the Western & Atlantic Railroad (W&A) stretching from Atlanta to Dalton to Chattanooga and beyond. Several other rail companies were in existence at the time. According to some reports, the W&A was nicknamed "Grandpa's Railroad" because if one wanted a job, he had to be "grandfathered" in by relatives working there. (L&N.)

16

By the time this photograph was taken (around the 1890s), the Marietta & North Georgia Railway was operating on standard-gauge track and enabling the transport of more rolling stock. Open cars called gondolas were used for hauling loose bulk such as coal and lumber. The gondola in the foreground of this photograph may contain ballast—crushed rock that provides stability and drainage along the tracks. Kennesaw Mountain looms in the background of this image. During the Battle of Kennesaw Mountain on June 27, 1864, Union general William Sherman plotted a frontal attack while Gen. Joseph Johnston's Confederate Army of Tennessee dug trenches in the rocky, steep woods. The loss of 3,000 Union men—compared to Johnson's 1,000 Confederate deaths—was not a tactical victory for Sherman, but he would press on in his determination to take down the Confederacy's railroads, suppliers, and manufacturers. (L&N.)

The Craigmiles, influential merchants in Cleveland, Tennessee, started many of the town's establishments during the Civil War and Reconstruction era. John Craigmiles came from Georgia in 1850, traveled west to California and made his fortune in shipping, and returned to Tennessee in 1857. John was on the board of commissioners that attempted to construct a railroad (Cleveland & Ducktown) between Cleveland and Georgia in the early 1850s; however, the company was not able to sell any stock to fund it, so they had to abandon the idea. John's brother Pleasant M. Craigmiles built Craigmiles House (pictured), an Italian villa–style home, in Cleveland in 1866 as a symbol of the South's rebirth after the war. (CBCPL.)

The Atlanta Lard Oil Factory, built along the railroad tracks in downtown Atlanta in 1864, came about as an example of industry progress in the area. Sidney Root and his partner, John Beach, made money in the dry goods business and also created three-story iron storefronts, which business owners preferred over wood. Root became politically influential with the Confederacy and ran blockades to acquire supplies from Europe; his tenacity led to the formation of the Board of Direct Trade, the predecessor of the Atlanta Chamber of Commerce. (LOC.)

Abel Stanhope Hill returned to Nottla Township, North Carolina, after the Civil War and served as sheriff of Cherokee County. After moving close to Ducktown, Tennessee, in 1878, he planned on selling farm produce to miners, but a recession caused mine closings, and clothing, food, and schooling became scarce. Abel's son Thomas J. Hill (born in 1878) attended the University of North Carolina and eventually became an attorney. Pictured above are, from left to right, Abel and Jane Rogers Hill and their children Luther, Mary, Arthur, Hattie, William Felix, Thomas, and Julius. (Thomas Panter III.)

James Madison Panter Jr., born in 1852, was a child in Rutherford County, North Carolina, when copper mining took off near Ducktown. He married Emma Sissum (pictured at right with James) and moved to Tennessee to farm. Several members of this family ended up working at the mines, including James Madison Panter III, who was killed on the job. (Thomas Panter III.)

The Hiwassee Loop, part of the Louisville & Nashville Railroad (L&N) route, runs due east toward Copperhill, Tennessee, crossing the Hiwassee River near Alliance and continuing along the gorge. As elevation rapidly increases, trains make a 360-degree circle around the mountain, rising 100 feet and passing under a 60-foot-high wooden trestle. Trains then round the mountain again—this time only 290 degrees—before gaining another 50 feet and stopping atop the trestle after crossing over the track and cresting at Farner. (Author's collection.)

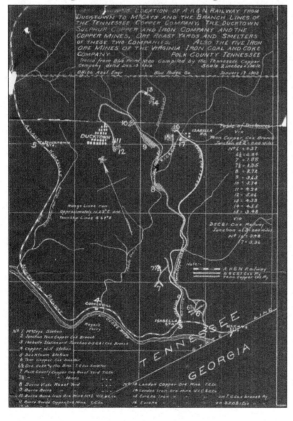

This January 1903 survey map of the Copper Basin shows the path of the Atlanta, Knoxville & Northern Railway north of Ducktown, where it follows the Ocoee River before arriving at McCays. Mines had small, private railroads with open cars that transported ore within the companies. Miners loaded cars at hoist points and then moved them to different processing areas. Workers loaded processed chemicals into company tank cars and filled hoppers and boxcars with copper for shipment. (DBM.)

The river known as "Toccoa" in Georgia becomes the Ocoee in Tennessee just over the state line at Copperhill. The Ocoee is an antecedent stream that maintains its northwesterly course in spite of changes in rock patterns within its depths. US Highway 64 follows the Ocoee beyond Ducktown toward Chattanooga. Highway 64 also follows the former dirt path of the Old Copper Road. (CBCPL.)

In the late 1800s, the community of Postelle, Tennessee, had a store, a school, a church, and two streets. People took buggy rides from the Postelle depot to Ducktown. John Hyatt (his position is indicated in the image) was the area mailman. He and an unidentified man and woman are shown standing at the Ducktown Station depot in 1891. (DBM.)

21

By the 1870s, trains were burning coal for fuel. Coal, plentiful in the eastern United States, is denser than wood and produces more energy per pound—about three times as much. This image shows a coal chute, located near the Cleveland depot, that supplied fuel for the Southern Railway locomotives that operated out of the depot. (CBCPL.)

German-born Julius Raht, whose management of Ducktown's early mines helped create the town, also had financial interest in Cleveland, where he founded a bank (pictured here around 1900 with a framed image of Raht above the tellers) and managed the Copper Road. In 1861, a man named Zulaski built a copper rolling mill (foundry) in Cleveland that used raw materials from Polk County mines. One of the products Zulaski designed around that time was explosive Confederate ammunition called a "Rebel torpedo." When the Union army heard about this, they hunted down the foundry and set it on fire, creating an enormous fireworks display. (CBCPL.)

Repair shops in Marietta and Blue Ridge serviced Marietta & North Georgia and Atlanta, Knoxville & Northern Railroad engines. In Blue Ridge around 1900, three engines could be repaired at a time in this shop on the far end of town near Ada Street. This shop closed when the Louisville & Nashville Railroad replaced the Old Line with the New Line in 1906, and the shops moved to the new town of Etowah. (L&N.)

James Knox Polk Cole (1842–1927; pictured), of the Hothouse community in Fannin County, owned a meat-packaging business along the tracks of Cole's Crossing, which was a railroad flag stop on the Murphy Branch line. Cole's Crossing was only a few miles from Mineral Bluff Depot. Cole married Nancy Louisa Brock in 1868, and they raised eight children together. He was also a notary public and a justice of the peace. The woman and children in the photograph are unidentified. (Mark and Linda Watkins Stewart.)

In 1900, tracks were laid or repaired near this neighborhood close to Atlanta. Maintenance was hard labor, with jacks used to correct vertical track issues and fix horizontal track movement. In the early days, "maintenance of way" workers slept in tents along the tracks. Prior to the 1880s, there were no boardinghouses for these workers. Eventually, necessitated by harsh weather, the workers began to use old railcars as bunk cars. (LOC.)

After cotton and tannery ventures, Joseph Winship built freight cars at his Atlanta ironworks, and his sons manufactured guns for Confederate troops. Pictured in 1889 in front of Winship's factory are, from left to right, Al Dobbs (Cartersville), Pat Mayson, Dan Hoy and Albert Richards (Nashville), Charles Robinson (Vinings), Walter Neal (Resaca), William Ray (Cartersville), Fred Robinson (Vinings), Jessie Orr (Resaca), Swan Ray (Cartersville), and Mike Mayson (Atlanta). The back of the photograph says: "Believed to have been employed by L&N." (Ana Bird Stokes.)

Two

Towns Blossom in Urban and Rural Georgia

"There are few things of greater interest to the citizen than the facilities for traveling, and getting the products of his industry to market. No man is willing to live in a country where he can leave home only at a great inconvenience and expense, or where he is compelled to consume a great part of the value of his produce in finding a purchaser."

—Thomas P. Janes, Commissioner, Georgia Department of Agriculture, 1876

In his 1876 publication *Handbook of the State of Georgia*, Janes listed 36 short line railroads and noted that 200 more miles of track were under construction. Most of these short-line railroads came and went, while some consolidated. The Marietta & North Georgia Railroad (M&NG) certainly had its fits and starts; by the time it made a connection with Knoxville Southern in 1890, the railroad was bankrupt.

The M&NG entered receivership in 1891, and in 1896, Atlanta, Knoxville & Northern Railway purchased it. During this transitional era, copper mining had experienced its own ups and downs. German engineer Julius Raht had arrived in Ducktown in the late 1850s; he managed mines, later became superintendent, and essentially built the town. All mining stopped during the Civil War. Afterward, Raht restarted the mines, but by the late 1870s, all mines had closed due—in large part—to lack of a railroad to transport ore economically. Everything changed with the arrival of the M&NG, and by the time the railroad's ownership changed, the mines were expanding and had a smelter.

The rebirth of mining provided employment for both locals and outsiders. As they toiled, their families grew, and the area's population boomed. Rail service in the mountains required depots, which became places people visited to ship products, receive supplies, gossip, retrieve mail, and venture beyond the confines of the town. Thanks to the arrival of trains, once-remote communities became little towns blooming near the railroads. A tannery and brickyard opened in Mineral Bluff, a quarry in the Kinsey community, and the area contained many boardinghouses.

In 1902, the mighty Louisville & Nashville Railroad purchased the M&NG train line. To many, this change seemed to signal exciting growth and improvements for the remote, mountainous area.

Confederate colonel Michael McKinney (1840–1925), whose father settled in what became Fannin County, rode horseback and walked the entire proposed Marietta & North Georgia Railroad (M&NG) route to what would become Blue Ridge. McKinney, a successful merchant, traveled long distances hauling his goods to markets. With surveyor C.R. Walton, he scouted sections and vehemently argued in favor of a railroad extending north. He and Walton platted the town of Blue Ridge, founding it in 1887—the same year the M&NG arrived. The men's homes were the first in Blue Ridge. This home, built by Col. McKinney's descendant Robert McKinney near Chestnut Gap/Fightingtown Creek, was recently restored and is all that remains of the McKinney holdings. (Author's collection.)

Gristmills were common sights in early north Georgia communities. Mills produced flour, meal, and sorghum that could be sold at market. In the 1880 census, farming was by far the dominant area occupation, but landowners often also had a logging business or a mill. Blue Ridge/Fannin County historians Dale Dyer and Danny Mashburn found evidence of and recorded over 140 gristmills in Fannin County. (Author's collection.)

The McKinney Mill was one of the largest mills in the area. The original mill that Michael McKinney purchased from the Hicks family was built at Chestnut Gap and later burned down by Union troops in 1864. Left with little, the McKinneys escaped to their old homestead in Roane County, Tennessee, but later returned and rebuilt at Chestnut Gap. The compound contained a store, a post office, entertainment (trained bears), and a weaving operation. The reminiscences of Hepsey McKinney, Michael's wife, about her husband's business corroborate a note in a 1928 government survey concerning the trading of local goods for necessities. Hepsey recalled that mountaineers traded beeswax, furs, venison, tallow, and dried herbs with her husband in exchange for merchandise. Prior to the arrival of the Marietta & North Georgia Railroad, McKinney would travel three days, by wagon, to Atlanta for goods. The mill ceased operations when a flood destroyed the dam in the 1930s. (FCHF.)

The Atlanta, Knoxville & Northern Railway (AK&N) operated for a total of nine years—from 1896 to 1905. It was a typical small-to-medium-sized Eastern railroad. The Louisville & Nashville acquired the railroad in 1902, but did not actually switch the name until 1905. AK&N had branches to marble quarries in Murphy and Tate. The men on the car at left in this image are sitting on large blocks of marble. (McClung-UT.)

A 1902 *Atlanta Constitution* article states that the Atlanta, Knoxville & Northern Railway's Knights of Pythias (a fraternal organization) and citizens of Blue Ridge had organized a Fourth of July celebration. It was to feature "antebellum times" festivities. Delegates from surrounding counties would be in attendance, and excursion trains from Ducktown and other points were planned. The event's planners were expecting "a great gathering of the mountain people" that would be "heartily" enjoyed. Sam W. Small of Blue Ridge was to be a guest speaker. This is a photograph of AK&N engineers at Blue Ridge in 1897. (DBM.)

Marble quarrying began in Pickens County prior to the Civil War. After the war, quarry owners enthusiastically supported the railroad entering the area. As with the Copper Basin, by 1880 the marble industry was defunct due to the lack of effective transport to markets. It restarted in 1883 when the Marietta & North Georgia Railroad arrived. In 1884, Samuel Tate opened the Georgia Marble Company in Pickens County, and the industry was reborn. The marble belt is approximately 60 miles long and stretches from Canton, Georgia, into Cherokee, North Carolina. This is Atlanta's neo-Gothic style city hall (the city's fourth), built in 1930 with white Georgia marble used on its balustrade and Mitchell Street entrance. (LOC.)

The Georgia State Capitol in downtown Atlanta, built during the Reconstruction period, was constructed of Indiana limestone and Georgia marble; the latter was used for its cornerstone, all interior floors and steps, and many walls. The sides of the second floor's walls are Etowah pink marble. The capitol building was completed in 1889. (LOC.)

Many US monuments, halls, libraries, banks, art centers, and stately homes were built from Georgia marble, which has also been sent all over the world for use in construction. The statue and plinth of the Lincoln Memorial (pictured) in Washington are Georgia white marble, and the pedestal and chamber floor are Tennessee pink marble. The US Capitol's 24 columns are Georgia marble. (LOC.)

By 1900, most Ducktown men worked in copper mines, and with trains running through Blue Ridge to Copperhill, all three towns prospered. The Louisville & Nashville clubhouse (pictured in the foreground) was built on pioneer Michael McKinney's deeded land in Blue Ridge. An 1899 *Atlanta Constitution* article announced that Atlanta, Knoxville & Northern Railway officials ordered plans drawn for the clubhouse with an estimated cost of $25,000. The clubhouse offered meals, billiard tables, baths, and other modern conveniences. (Ron Henry Collection.)

The first Blue Ridge Hotel (the building at left) was a wooden structure next to the brick Blue Ridge Pharmacy in what was called the Louisville & Nashville Railroad (L&N) Building, which was assumedly used for the railroad's offices. The brick building is now home to Coldwell Banker Realty, and the hotel burned down. (Ron Henry Collection.)

The second Blue Ridge Hotel went up on the same site as the original. This time, it sported a handsome cupola. It also burned down. A third Blue Ridge Hotel on the same site suffered the same fate; it was the last of the Blue Ridge Hotels. (Ron Henry Collection.)

Steam engines have a magical pull for some people even today. Their distinctive whistles, the chug of the wood-burning engines sending soot and cinders into the air, and the puffs of steam from the stacks bring back fond memories. This large Louisville & Nashville Railroad engine served the mountain area. (L&N.)

The crew pictured here in Blue Ridge seems ready for work. One man holds a hammer and another holds a broom. Some railroad employees lived in houses in Blue Ridge owned by the Louisville & Nashville Railroad; the small bungalow homes on Ada Street, built in the early 1900s, have been referred to as "Calico Houses." They were located a short walk away from the train tracks and repair shops. (Ron Henry Collection.)

This group of well-dressed ladies looks excited about a trip they are about to embark on or have just taken. People came from many places to partake of Blue Ridge's mineral springs, while local ladies also day-tripped to Atlanta for shopping, returning to Blue Ridge in the late afternoon. (FCHF.)

James Madison Panter III (fourth from left), born to James Madison Panter Jr. and Emma Sissum in 1887, worked for Louisville & Nashville Railroad as a rock feeder. He was killed at age 31 when he accidentally got caught in the belt of a rock breaker and was thrown against a post. (Thomas Panter III.)

Bennett Franklin Womble (shown at left with his family) worked for the Louisville & Nashville (L&N) Railroad, but not for long. He preferred farming and eventually went to work at a sawmill in Tellico Plains, Tennessee. Bennett's brother, Joseph Pittgreer Womble, stayed with L&N. He started as a laborer, became a foreman, and worked with the company for over 30 years before retiring in the 1930s. Joseph's son Thomas Wesley Womble (standing beside his father in the below image) followed in his footsteps and was an L&N timekeeper in the 1920s. (Both, Cindy Womble Billman.)

Dr. Lucius Ezell Kimsey (pictured) practiced medicine in Ducktown for 50 years and was a proponent of constructing a road in nearby Little Frog Mountain Wilderness, which is considered wilderness for a reason. Few people lived there, and in an odd juxtaposition of those who did, a postal worker trapped in a blizzard froze to death, and a little girl burned to death in a house fire; they are buried near each other. When the 15-mile Kimsey Highway was completed in 1916, it spiraled from its southernmost access at the Greasy Creek community to the Harbuck community, four miles north of Ducktown. Dr. Kimsey was the first one to drive along the highway. (Sarah McWhorter.)

Kimsey Highway, once considered one of the nation's greatest roadways, attracted many tourists. Once the superhighways were built, the popularity of the steep, winding, single-track road rapidly declined. Today, Little Frog Mountain (aka Kimsey Mountain) is inhabited by deer, turkey, bear, snakes, and other wildlife. Kimsey Highway draws nature lovers, motorcyclists, and other adventure-seekers to its dirt-and-gravel road with pretty clearings, creeks, and waterfalls. (DBM.)

John Jay Crawford, pictured here around 1908 with his two daughters, Maude (on his lap) and Inez, was a deputy sheriff and notary public from Morganton, Georgia, who later became a Louisville & Nashville Railroad patrolman—this type of job often went to local authorities. He and wife, Vandora, had seven children. Of those, Everett worked for R.J. Reynolds Tobacco Company and wrote crossword puzzles for the *New York Times*. Howell became an Atlanta architect. US Army second lieutenant Donald retired from the Pentagon. William taught school locally and at the Military Institute of Georgia. The youngest, Stella, also taught school. (Lynne Tipton.)

Young Sam Craig (left) is standing next to a man identified only as Mason. Craig (1893–1964) was a mine and safety engineer with the Tennessee Copper Company. They are pictured here wearing mining lights and heavy boots and carrying large wrenches. Craig was general mine foreman when the Tennessee Copper Company made a connection of drift from Boyd Mine and Cherokee shaft in 1960, which gave them access to the newest ore body. (Sue Craig Taylor.)

The Louisville & Nashville Railroad built the Copperhill depot in the area below the Tennessee Copper Company's Smelter Hill, where a small produce stand now sets up shop. Today, the location is across Georgia State Route 60 from the Ocoee River, but the highway was not there when the depot existed. In this photograph, several horses and wagons stand near the depot while a few people sit on the riverbank. (DBM.)

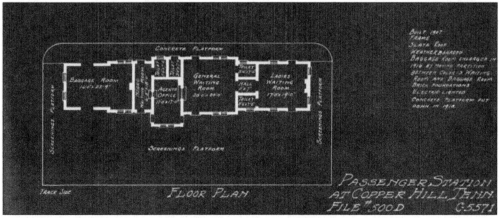

This 1907 blueprint of the Copperhill depot—with its separate "Negro waiting room"—illustrates one aspect of segregation during the Jim Crow era. At that time, and continuing into the 1960s, many Southern states upheld laws ordering businesses to keep clientele separated according to race. The diagram also shows a "ladies waiting room" at the far end of the building. (L&N.)

The Copperhill depot is pictured here around 1906. The depot was eventually torn down after cars became popular, necessitating the highway. Colonial Hotel owner George Hood was a Louisville & Nashville Railroad agent before building and opening the two-story hotel to the right of this depot in 1914. At that time, six trains ran through per day, including one to Atlanta and one to Knoxville. The Atlanta train spent the night in Knoxville, and the Knoxville train spent the night in Murphy. Hood regularly sent a bellhop over to the trains to inform passengers that the hotel rented rooms just across the street. (DBM.)

Railroads required places for workers to stay while performing various duties and would often put them up in local hotels or boardinghouses. Mine employees also frequented these establishments. This two-story wooden structure is believed to be a hotel or boardinghouse in Ducktown. (Lynne Tipton.)

Three

THE SYMBIOSIS OF RAILROAD AND TOWN

As the 19th century transitioned into the 20th, railroad transportation surged forward. Improved equipment, better routes, and a move toward standardization hastened progress. The Atlanta-to-Knoxville route's cumbersome "W" switchback had been replaced with the Hiwassee Loop and accommodated a rise in ore loads. Nearby marble quarries, logging, and textile industries took advantage of railroads hauling local goods to outlying markets, thereby increasing profits.

During this era of economic and industrial development, Ball Ground, Georgia, was illustrative of how towns developed as a direct result of railroad access. In 1882, the Marietta & North Georgia Railroad surveyed the area and wanted to build a depot and town. Local landowners deeded acreage for its use, stating: "The consideration moving each of us in the establishing of this town is the enhanced value to our lands within and adjacent to the said town, and the general benefit to the country, by which we shall be benefited."

When the railroad parceled town lots and offered them for sale in April 1882, people snapped them up. Two years later, Ball Ground had approximately 259 citizens, several new buildings, three churches, a high school, a charter, and municipal officers.

By 1900, the same could be said of Ducktown, Isabella, and Copperhill in the Copper Basin, as well as nearby Blue Ridge and Mineral Bluff. Copper mining had brought growth—improved methods of extracting and processing ore meant profits and job security. Undertakers, bankers, lawyers, city officials, accountants, and many railroad employees inhabited the towns along with miners, farmers, preachers, teachers, innkeepers, tradesmen, and merchants.

In 1906, the Louisville & Nashville Railroad built the New Line between Etowah, Tennessee, and Cartersville, Georgia, to bypass the Hiwassee Loop so that freight could move faster and more smoothly. This helped the copper mines, which had opened a sulfuric acid plant in 1907.

In spite of the progress, the mountains remained much the same in many ways. Most families worked small, inherited farms. Work was done by hand or with one- or two-horse plows. What could not be grown or made was acquired by trade; people had access to supplies from local rock quarries, brickyards, tanneries, and gristmills. Lumber mills were plentiful, numbering around 2,000 in Georgia by 1910. Outsider timber speculators purchased old farmland and created settlements in parts of North Carolina, Tennessee, and northern Georgia, providing some logging camp jobs.

As the new century dawned, big business had to interact with pioneer ways, and they became at once dependent and independent of each other.

A bird's-eye view from across the Ocoee River shows the Louisville & Nashville Railroad's Copperhill depot surrounded by passengers and cars. The Colonial Hotel is to the right of the station. About nine miles away, following the Old Copper Road west before cutting almost due north, Calvin and Amanda Higdon heard the railroad was coming. In 1890, they built the Higdon Hotel near the tracks to house their family, railroad employees, and travelers. The railroad men called this stop Higdon's Station, although the community's postal stop was known as Reliance. The family also operated Higdon's Ferry to transport visitors across the Hiwassee River until a road was built in 1912. The Higdons ran their hotel until 1920. The Higdon Hotel still stands in the Reliance Historic District. (Ron Henry Collection.)

This Ducktown High School girls' basketball team sat for a photographer in 1916 in uniforms that included bows and bloomers. At that time, women's basketball teams would play or defend one-third of the court and could have six players on the court at any time. Stealing the ball was considered unladylike. In the early 1900s and 1910s, women were not allowed to dribble the ball. After 1918, the game rules for women's basketball became more similar to those of men's basketball. (FCHF.)

The Mineral Bluff depot is the oldest public building in Fannin County and the only remaining Marietta & North Georgia Railroad depot. Built in 1887 using local bricks, it is listed in the National Register of Historic Places. John Nichols grew up hearing from elderly relatives about how everyone came out for the train's 3:00 p.m. stop in anticipation of the newspaper delivery, after which someone would read the daily reports to the crowd. (Patricia Hardin.)

This c. 1914 image shows the Louisville & Nashville Railroad passenger station in Copperhill. The station existed until passenger service ended in 1951, when it was torn down. According to the January 20, 1972, issue of the *McCaysville Citizen*, four trains came to Copperhill each day in 1922. Howard Hood, son of Colonial Hotel owner George Hood, told the *Citizen* that he used to take sandwiches to the station to sell to the passengers. (DBM.)

In 1905, two Galloway brothers were killed on an Louisville & Nashville Railroad (L&N) excursion train. J.L. (a local tax collector) had words with a train agent, presumably over a broken car window. According to the *Atlanta Constitution*, J.L. exited to another car, returning with his brother G.W., and a fight ensued. Captain Ewing, the train's conductor, was stabbed several times before fatally shooting the brothers. J.L.'s widow sued, Captain Ewing was found innocent, and Judge Gober ruled for L&N on damages. Similar area train fatalities included the following: "Oddfellow Poly Franklon was killed by a reck [sic] on the train June 23, 1905"; "Charley Pack was killed on L&N RR May 18, 1912"; "Buddy Hooper was killed by falling off the train August 10 1912"; and "Andy Styles was killed by a train Aug 6, 1923 in North Athens, TN." (Both, author's collection.)

According to relatives, George Abernathy held the first mortician's license in Georgia. The Center and Abernathy general mercantile store and funeral parlor offered Ducktown miners "furniture, coffins and caskets." Abernathy's son, Luther, opened a second furniture store in Copperhill, Tennessee, and by the 1930s, Abernathy's advertised furniture via a billboard set against the Copper Basin's bare hills. After enduring fires and rebuilding, Abernathy's Complete Home Furnishings remains in operation north of Blue Ridge, where its catchy slogan—"you marry the girl, we'll furnish the home"—still beckons customers. (Ron Henry Collection.)

The Tennessee Copper Company built a YMCA for employees and their families that offered boarding for area workers and contained a gym, a flower shop, a barbershop, a bowling alley, a library, and a café. The YMCA hosted events such as movies, square dances, school carnivals, and skating. Professional wrestlers from Chattanooga made appearances there. "Uncle" George Freeman, minister of Mine City Baptist Church, was its director. (Ron Henry Collection.)

In this c. 1910 photograph taken in Bartow County, a group of workmen are standing beside a row of cars. The county contained a garage for car repairs in Calhoun, 30 miles north of Cartersville, as well as a car dealership in downtown Cartersville. (Samuel McMillan Freeman.)

Cartersville, Georgia, is 44 miles northwest of Atlanta and 76 miles southeast of Chattanooga. It was incorporated in 1859 upon the arrival of the Western & Atlantic Railroad. When the railroad's depot was remodeled in 1902, workers discovered several old railroad items—including this baggage claim ticket from a trip between Rome and Cartersville—within its walls. The depot's segregated ticket windows and waiting rooms remain a part of the building, which now houses the Cartersville Welcome Center. The depot did not come out of the Civil War unscathed, as evidenced by a bullet hole in its brick outer wall. (City of Cartersville.)

N. C. & ST. L. RY.

191.....

RELEASE

The Nashville, Chattanooga & St. Louis Ry. having consented to carry my baggage (bearing check number as shown hereon) which I acknowledge to be in condition as designated by cross (X) mark on back hereof,

FROM

Cartersville

TO

Rome Ga

I hereby release and forever discharge the said Nashville, Chattanooga & St. Louis Ry. and all other transportation companies over which my baggage may be handled on this check, from all liability for any damage, or loss which may happen to said baggage while in their possession.

....
Owner.
....
Address.

A 42357
BAD ORDER

The Louisville & Nashville Railroad's "rules and instructions" were issued yearly in small clothbound books such as this 1909 booklet found during the Cartersville depot renovations. One of its front pages contains a company statement that says: "A Careful, thoughtful employe [sic] does not need a sign as a reminder that safety is of first importance in the discharge of duty." (City of Cartersville.)

This typewritten letter—dated 1913 and found during Cartersville's station renovation—shows claims agent S.D. Cowden asking depot agent J.H. Wofford about lost freight. An 1894 city directory lists Santford D. Cowden as a clerk for the East Tennessee, Virginia, & Georgia Railway, which was later incorporated into Southern Railway. The freight in question was a rock crusher sent by the John G. Duncan Company. In 1886, Duncan was vice president of the newly formed J.M. Greer & Company of Knoxville, Tennessee, which sold both steam and horse-powered threshers. (City of Cartersville.)

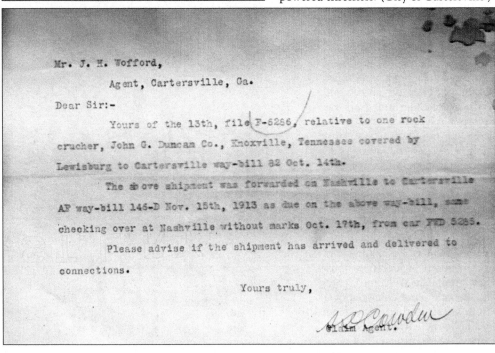

This old record book, dated 1928, lists the engine as No. 316. A number of names are written at the top of the page are on the line for "Foreman." "W. Donahue" is unidentified, but the others were found in a 1940 census. Steve B. Gilstrap, born around 1890, was a conductor and rented a room in Cartersville; in 1928, he was 38 years old. Lindsey L. Gilstrap, his fireman, was 46 in 1928 and owned a house in Cartersville. The column heading "Seals" contains places. Alto and Acworth are 90 minutes apart. At various stops, the crew picked up freight at houses and mills. (City of Cartersville.)

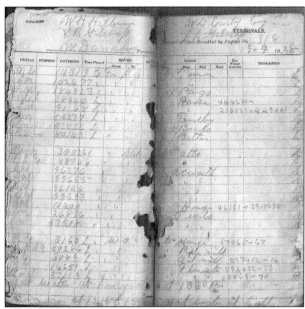

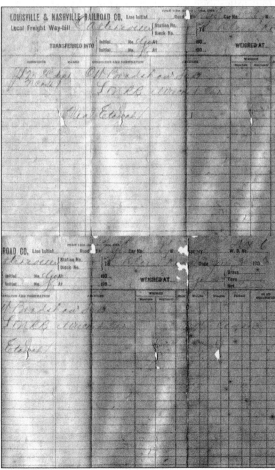

The train repair shops moved from Blue Ridge to Etowah in 1906. This freight record from July 1906 was for a wrecked Louisville & Nashville Railroad car going from Cartersville to Blue Ridge and assumedly on to Etowah. Waybills, kept by the conductor for each freight car, gave details and instructions for a shipment, showed the freight's destination and arrival record, and specified the railroad to which the car belonged. (City of Cartersville.)

The depot in Tate, Georgia, built in 1916, was in continuous use into the 1940s. At one time, this depot was one of the busiest on the Old Line. The marble vein that stretches across it is a solid block three-eighths of a mile wide, four miles long, and up to a half-mile deep. Georgia Marble Company began in Pickens County in 1884. From 1905 to 1938, Sam Tate (grandson of company founder Sam Tate) served as president of Georgia Marble, the largest company in the area, and employed local citizens. His power plant made Tate the first town in the area with electricity. Even after a century of quarry excavation, by the 1970s, only a few acres of marble had been removed. (L&N.)

In 1924, a Louisville & Nashville Railroad publication called *Lively Lines* quoted engineer Sid A. Garwood on why he liked his job. He replied that safety measures were well observed by everyone down the line. Garwood, along with his two brothers, worked for the railroad for many years. His brother Bill brought the "Little Mary" steam engine into Ellijay and Blue Ridge on the railroad's first runs in those towns. In the early 1900s, Bill built a home in Blue Ridge, where he lived until the shops closed and new ones were built in Etowah. Sid brought the first train into Etowah on December 6, 1906. (L&N.)

SOUTHERN SCHOOL OF TELEGRAPHY

To all to whom these presents may come, Greeting:

This Certifies that _S. J. Freeman_ has completed the regular course of study and practice in

TELEGRAPHY AND TYPEWRITING

as prescribed by this Institution, and upon examination is found competent to properly transmit and receive twenty-five words per minute, and has demonstrated a thorough knowledge of all the details pertaining to Commercial and Railway Telegraphy. The recipient has therefore been pronounced worthy of graduation and entitled to receive this

Diploma

with the same all the honors due to superior attainments and correct deportment, and we hereby recommend the holder to the favorable consideration of the public.

In Testimony Whereof, We have hereunto subscribed our names and affixed the seal of this Institution, in the Executive Office at Newnan, Georgia, this _19th_ day of _March_ Nineteen Hundred and _fifteen_

_____ President _____ Superintendent

Samuel Jackson Freeman worked on the Louisville & Nashville Railroad's New Line from his youth until he retired in 1962. In 1915, he attended the Southern School of Telegraphy in Newnan, Georgia, south of Atlanta. Such educational training was required for depot agents, who sent telegraphs in Morse code. The first time Samuel Morse's telegraph was used for dispatching in railroading was in 1851. Freeman was a depot agent in several different towns throughout his career, sending and receiving both train-related telegraph messages and Western Union messages. (Samuel McMillan Freeman.)

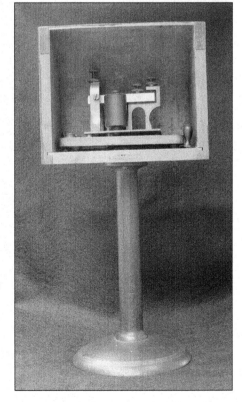

Samuel J. Freeman's telegraph receiver (pictured) was his pride and joy. This was his main tool in his job at the depot; depot agents were constantly busy jotting notes and making sure they were received by trains as they passed. The depot agent's job was of the utmost importance, since he helped in the movement of trains. At first, depot agents extended dispatch sticks that allowed handwritten dispatches to be snatched by those inside the train as it passed the depot. If the dispatch was missed, the train had to be stopped and reversed—a time-consuming and undesirable alternative. (Samuel McMillan Freeman.)

Telegraph operator Samuel J. Freeman (right) and his coworker S.C. "Skid" Jones stand in front of the Delano depot, located just outside Etowah on the Louisville & Nashville Railroad's New Line. The depots were manned around the clock. If traffic was heavy, they would have second and third "tricks" (shifts). Depot agents received payment on freight, sold tickets to passengers, issued bills of lading for outgoing freight, and ordered cars for outgoing shipments. (Samuel McMillan Freeman.)

Standing in front of a Railway Express cart at the Delano depot are Samuel J. Freeman (left), S.C. "Skid" Jones (center), and J.E. McMillan (Freeman's brother-in-law). The grids in the depot's windows are anti-thievery devices. The Railway Express, used to haul small packages that did not need large baggage cars, was similar to modern delivery services. (Samuel McMillan Freeman.)

Samuel McMillan Freeman, shown here in his US Navy uniform, was born in 1927. When he was a boy, his family lived in White, Georgia, a town along the Louisville & Nashville (L&N) Railroad's New Line. Now 87, he has wonderful memories of his father's career with the L&N. He remembers living close to the tracks and how the house vibrated when the train passed. He loved the steam engine's whistle but found the newer diesel engine's whistle disappointing. (Samuel McMillan Freeman.)

As an L&N depot agent, Samuel J. Freeman wore a suit, vest, and tie each day, and he always had a pistol. In the heat of summer, he would remove his vest and jacket. When handing up orders to the train, he would put his cap on. He made notes for dispatches on a carbon-copy notepad with a copying pencil. This photograph, showing a young Freeman (right), was taken at what appears to be a rock quarry. (Patricia Hardin.)

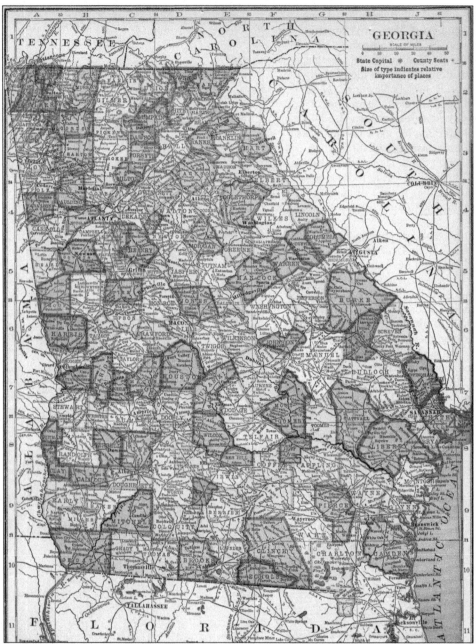

A 1910 Georgia map from C.S. Hammond & Company's *Hammond's Modern Atlas of the World*, compiled from government surveys, includes several towns along both the Old Line and New Line of the Louisville & Nashville (L&N) Railroad, as well as other important connections. Since "size of type indicates relative importance of places," according to the cartographer, prominent places along the railroad are discernible. Atlanta is written in the largest print, followed by Chattanooga (in Tennessee), Dalton, Cartersville, and Marietta. Blue Ridge is in medium-sized print. Towns lists in small print include Cleveland, Apalachia, Murphy, Sweetgum, McCays, Mineral Bluff, Ellijay, Jasper, Etowah, Fairmount, Canton, Ball Ground, Woodstock, Toonigh, and Holly Springs. (Author's collection.)

54

A staged advertisement from 1909 shows a surprised Pullman porter observing a loving couple. The man has bestowed flowers on his sweetheart while another group of passengers looks on approvingly. This image is indicative of the "golden age" of rail travel in the United States, which lasted for nearly the entire first half of the 20th century. (LOC.)

This c. 1905 image shows Henry Marshall Cole, stationmaster, seated in his Louisville & Nashville (L&N) Railroad office in Knoxville, Tennessee. The man standing behind him is unidentified. The L&N passenger station—a vast presence on Western Avenue in downtown Knoxville—was designed by engineer Richard Monfort and rivaled the Southern Railway station on Depot Street. The station's brick structure with stone detailing and clay-tiled peaked roofs is considered both châteauesque and Victorian in style. The majestic station opened in April 1905. L&N's last passenger train left the station in 1968. (McClung-UT.)

L&N completed their station at the Knoxville freight yard in 1904. At the time, the railroad was both offering passenger service and moving massive amounts of freight, including pulpwood for paper factories and coal and lumber for logging companies, throughout the South. (McClung-UT.)

Four

TRAINS, HOMETOWN FOLK, AND VISITORS

A 1928 Department of Agriculture Soil Survey of Fannin County opens with an overall view of the extreme north Georgia region, wherein the survey writers, S.W. Phillips and J.W. Stephenson (both from the Georgia State College of Agriculture), conclude that the region has prospered much in the two previous decades.

By the time the survey was conducted, Blue Ridge was home to the sprawling Willingham Girls School, the state Baptist assembly grounds, a hardware store, the passenger and freight depot, a bank, hotels, movie theaters, a restaurant, and a bedspread factory.

In 1920, Blue Ridge's population was 904 while McCaysville's was 2,166. The latter town had become a local trade center for farm produce, and most of its residents worked at the mines. Copperhill's population was 1,102 in 1920.

Blue Ridge enticed summer visitors with its mild climate, and its mineral springs attracted many people in partaking of its purported healing waters. Mineral Bluff was a trade and shipping center for other parts of Fannin County, along with other minor trading centers Fry, Morganton, Epworth, and Sweetgum.

Etowah was the Louisville & Nashville (L&N) Railroad's main line connection north to Knoxville and Cincinnati, while Marietta was the main connection to Atlanta and points south. Several trains came through the towns each day. Agriculture was still Etowah's main industry, with many small farms worked by families. Extra labor only paid about $1 a day, and most chose to work in the mines, plants, public works, or lumber companies. The survey writer noted that before moving to Etowah, the train shops in Blue Ridge had been a place where farmers sold excess produce; they also sold to local markets and at lumber camps and copper mines.

Hydroelectric power entered the area with the construction of the Blue Ridge Dam, which the Toccoa Electric Power Company built between 1925 and 1930. The dam generated electricity for the growing population, and it did not contribute pollution to the area, so there was little opposition to the project.

When the Louisville & Nashville Railroad connected Knoxville and Atlanta, it opened up trade potential between the two cities and beyond, since the railroad stretched as far north as Cincinnati and St. Louis. In this 1919 photograph, the train is following the Tennessee River (which follows the old Dixie Highway) as it rounds the mountain between Knoxville and Chattanooga. (McClung-UT.)

In 1956, this large crowd assembled at the depot in celebration of Etowah's 50th Jubilee. Depots often served as gathering places where locals could catch up on the news, gossip, travel, and pick up mail and packages. The local passenger train from Cartersville to Etowah was called the "Short Dog." (Ron Henry Collection.)

In this January 1926 image taken in Knoxville, a large group of Louisville & Nashville (L&N) Railroad crew members have assembled at the roundhouse, which is a locomotive maintenance shed built around a turntable. In the early years of the railroads, steam engines—plus some other rolling stock—could only move forward. The trains did not have a mechanical capacity for reversing, and even when they were altered so that they could move backward, it was often too difficult to reverse an entire train. Turntables made it relatively simple for trains to be turned around for return trips. Blue Ridge did not have a turntable when it had its repair shops. The shops in Etowah, which were much larger, did have a turntable. (McClung-UT.)

This railroad crew pictured at the Blue Ridge Depot in 1926 or 1927 included, from left to right, Jack Walker (flagman), unidentified, ? Jenkins (brakeman), Jule Adams (conductor), and Sam Nix (fireman). (FCHF.)

Toccoa Dam, now known as the Blue Ridge Dam, is a hydroelectric facility just outside of the town of Blue Ridge, Georgia. The Toccoa Electric Power Company, a subsidiary of the Tennessee Electric Power Company, began construction on the dam in 1925 and completed it in 1930. The Toccoa Electric Power Company later sold the dam to the Tennessee Valley Authority. Several local homesteads had to be removed prior to the building of the dam. A side rail track was built out of Blue Ridge to transport materials used for building the dam and powerhouse; the small engines used were comparable to trains used on branches in the copper yards, marble quarries, and lumberyards. (TVA.)

This is Hamilton Fox's home on the Wall land tract in Dial, Georgia. An 1880 census shows he lived with his mother, siblings, aunt, and grandmother. The 1920 records list Fox as a 52-year-old general farmer. In a 1928 government land survey, a geologist notes that farmers in this area mostly had small cabins for houses, and that the farm buildings were small. Farmers worked the land using one- or two-horse (or mule) plows or tillers. This home was removed after a land survey that occurred prior to 1925, when construction began on the Blue Ridge Dam. (TVA.)

J.H. Weaver's home, on the Bailey land tract, was also surveyed and removed before the construction of the dam. In the 1940 census, Weaver is listed as 42, married, and having seven children. He rented a home on Noontootla Road in Blue Ridge and was listed as a farmer. A geologist working on the 1928 government land survey noted that farmers in Fannin County mainly raised subsistence crops. If the yield was more than the farmer's family could use, some sold their excess produce to men in the mines and lumber camps. (TVA.)

Surveyors working on the Blue Ridge Dam also looked at this Stony Battery quartz formation, which was surveyed prior to the construction of the dam. This quartz may have been used in the building of the dam. A quarry existed in the Hemptown community, east of Blue Ridge. There is an old quarry around Aska Road, close to Lake Blue Ridge and the dam, where the Masons hold annual large meetings. Rock formations were plentiful in Fannin County and required demolition, if necessary, for the progress of large infrastructure projects (such as the dam). (TVA.)

After the Blue Ridge Dam was finished in 1930, the locals were ready to celebrate. A Fourth of July picnic and barbecue held in downtown Blue Ridge included much fanfare and decoration. Willa Haight, who was active in the Blue Ridge community, is sitting in her car in the foreground of this photograph. Haight was a rider in the first car that drove across the dam. Her father, William C. Allen, bought a home in Blue Ridge in 1910 and worked at the train shops before running a furniture and hardware store. (FCHF.)

The year "1926" is visible on one of the license plates shown in this photograph of the crowded Louisville & Nashville Railroad station in Knoxville. The peak year for passenger train travel in the United States was 1920. As train usage reached 1.2 billion customers, ticket-buyers accepted a rate increase of 20 percent. At the same time, automobile usage had increased threefold. By 1929, passenger train travel had dropped by 18 percent. (McClung-UT.)

LOUISVILLE & NASHVILLE RAILROAD COMPANY

TRIP PASS

1927   (SUBJECT TO CONDITIONS ON BACK) NOT GOOD ON TRAINS Nos. 37, 38, 98, 99, 198 AND 199   N? 119588

PASS Miss Stella Crawford--------
-Not good on Trains 17 and 18----
ACCOUNT Dept. dtr of J.J.Crawford, Patrolman

To   Blue Ridge, Ga. FROM   Etowah, Tenn.

DATE ISSUED May 10th, 1927 GOOD FOR ONE TRIP ONLY, UNTIL June 15th, 1927

ADDRESS   Morganton, Ga REQUESTED BY   cds

VALID ONLY WHEN COUNTERSIGNED BY   M. SEARGEANT

COUNTERSIGNED BY   GENERAL MANAGER

FORM 3.

Stella, the daughter of railroad detective John Jay Crawford, of Morganton, Georgia, had a ticket to ride the train from Blue Ridge to Etowah—a distance of 62 miles—on a day between May 10 and June 15, 1927. Stella was from Morganton, a town six miles from Blue Ridge that was chartered in 1902 and was the county seat (before it moved to Blue Ridge after that city acquired the train). In 1900, Morganton's population was 115. (Lynne Tipton.)

Stella Crawford was the only child of John Jay Crawford's seven who remained in Fannin County her whole life. She taught school before marrying John Mosley. The Crawford family was the first in Fannin County to have a telephone. Stella's mother, Dora, was a member of the Baugh family, owners of a brickyard in Mineral Bluff, and Dora helped make and carry the bricks used to build the first Baptist church in Morganton. (Lynne Tipton.)

The Mary P. Willingham School for Girls, which was in operation from 1916 to 1931, was a private Baptist girls' school in Blue Ridge. The school taught grades seven through twelve. Six girls graduated the first year the school was open, but it grew, and by 1923, the school had 143 students and 34 graduates. Uniforms were required, as demonstrated in this photograph. (FCHF.)

Girls came to the Willingham School from different towns and surrounding states and attended classes with local students. When the out-of-town boarders arrived on the train, they were less than a mile from campus. The hack shown here was their ride. The term "hack" originated in England, where it was used in reference to taxicab drivers. (FCHF.)

Emma Lazelle married Oscar C. Beam in 1908, when they were 22 and 24, respectively, and they had a son and daughter. In the 1940 census, Oscar is 54 and his occupation is recorded as railway postal clerk. Emma, 52, is listed as a photographer and had her own home studio in Blue Ridge. The image at left shows an unidentified woman who was photographed in Emma's studio; she is wearing a sailor dress, which was the uniform at the Mary P. Willingham School for Girls, so she was likely a student there. (Author's collection.)

Billy Butler raised his family on land near Turtletown, Tennessee, seven miles north of Ducktown. He had a wife, Lou, and a daughter named Amy "Sis" Byrd. Billy farmed and made moonshine. The stacked crates shown at left are most likely for moonshine. Pictured here are, from left to right, Dan (Billy's son), Billy, Mary Helen (Billy's granddaughter), Lou, Vina Lou (Billy's granddaughter), and Lucy (Billy's daughter-in-law). Not pictured is Owen Byrd (related to Billy through marriage) who, as family lore goes, "hoboed" the train in Copperhill to get flour for his mother. He tried to get off just past Postelle so he could walk home, but by the time he could safely jump, he was in Harbuck; he then undertook a long walk home toting a 20-pound bag of flour. (Steve Byrd.)

James Sidney Curtis, pictured in his World War I uniform, was a career railroad employee who lived along the northern Georgia Louisville & Nashville line his entire life. Born in 1889, Curtis was born to North Carolina pioneers who took advantage of treaty-acquired Cherokee land. He married Ethel Mae Dooley of Cherokee County, Georgia, and the family resided at Tennessee Avenue in Etowah. Curtis was employed as a brakeman, charged with inspecting equipment and helping with train switching. By the time of the 1930 census, Curtis and his family had moved to Blue Ridge. After Ethel's death in 1935, he married Alice Pickett Maulding. They lived in Marietta until his death in 1966. (Joe Bob Long.)

These Tennessee Copper Company (TCC) employees took a photograph in April 1933 to celebrate the fact that the railway department had been accident-free for two years. Beginning in 1949, TCC gave their employees cans of coffee as rewards for achieving high safety standards; by 1953, they had awarded over 100,000 one-pound cans. (DBM.)

Elisha Panter (1890–1950) is perched on a Tennessee Copper Company train. According to family, he was a "peck" on the train. The meaning of this title is unclear. It may have been company jargon for "loader," based on commercial loading equipment with the same name. (Thomas Panter III.)

This 1922 photograph shows a part-Cherokee family from Monroe County, North Carolina. They were working at a logging camp when a man came by with a camera and asked if he could take their picture. Pictured here are, from left to right, (first row) Nettie Martin, Hattie Martin, Ethel Dovie Kirkland (holding Homer), and Avaline Orr; (second row) Williams Johns Martin, George Martin, Elbert Martin, and Avery Martin (holding Eva). Hattie got so excited that she took out her braids. (Candace West.)

In this 1940s image, Fred "Jack" Lee Botts, born in Fannin County in 1902, is shown holding an auction in his Botts Furniture & Appliance Store in McCaysville; Botts is in the foreground (at far left, in the white shirt with arm outstretched, taking a bid). He and his first wife, Alma Miller, owned and ran the store until around 1950. It was located near the steel bridge on the grounds that later served as the location for Williamson's Five and Dime. Botts opened similar stores in Albany, Georgia, and Melbourne, Florida. (Botts family.)

Lucius Burger, born in Isabella, Tennessee, in 1893, worked at London Mill, an extraction plant, or separating (flotation) and concentrating facility, where workers crushed copper ore, which was ground until it was superfine. The minerals were then separated. (Thomas Panter III.)

Flowers in hand, Lucius Burger is ready for a date. He is standing in front of one of the first Ford Model T cars in the Copperhill area. Lucius's father, William, was listed in the 1920 census as having two occupations: blacksmith and copper miner. (Thomas Panter III.)

Dorothy Burger was born in 1924 in the old Adam Burger cabin in the mining town of Isabella, Tennessee. She was a gospel singer, performing on the local radio station for over 20 years. She married Johnny Bandy (pictured at right with Dorothy) on July 19, 1942. He fought in World War II under Gen. George Patton and, afterward, worked at the copper plant where Dorothy's father, Lucius, worked. According to Dorothy's nephew, who gave her eulogy, neighbors down the street could hear Dorothy's cries for Johnny not to leave her as he lay dying; he died in her arms in 1974. She kept his pictures in her room and his shoes and clothing in her closet until the day she died in 2009. They did not have any children. (Thomas Panter III.)

This rundown Georgia gristmill is reminiscent of a time when most of the state was agrarian, and most people (as demonstrated by the 1880 Fannin County census) were farmers. This 1935 photograph is indicative of how hard the Great Depression hit the country. The photograph was taken for a project by the US Resettlement Administration, part of Pres. Franklin D. Roosevelt's New Deal. The Resettlement Administration's concept was to move massive amounts of rural and urban poor off of overworked land, out of poverty-stricken areas, and into planned communities (as depicted in John Steinbeck's *The Grapes of Wrath*). Since the resettlement program was unpopular in Congress, its scope was greatly reduced, with work completed mainly in California and Southern states, including parts of Georgia such as Eatonton, Gainesville, and Cornelia. (LOC.)

Author William Faulkner recognized the importance of religion in the South. Upon being asked why the subject appeared so often in his novels, he replied, "it's just there." Outdoor baptisms and revivals, like this one in Ducktown in 1930, were tied to the environment, and crowds would leave chores and work behind to support loved ones while seeking a refreshment of their own souls. (Steve Byrd.)

The Louisville & Nashville Railroad chose Etowah because it was a good spot to establish a railroad station. Engineer Sidney A. Garwood, of Euclid Avenue in Atlanta, is shown standing with his feet crossed. The other men are unidentified. This engine was scrapped in 1938. (L&N.)

CSX now owns the Hiwassee River Railroad Bridge (pictured), an all-verticals bridge with a Warren truss. It spans the Hiwassee River near Benton, Tennessee, and is still usable. This type of bridge superstructure was patented in 1848 by James Warren and Willoughby T. Monzani. Its equilateral triangle spaces are a simple, economical design that reduces strain on any one part. Warren trusses have also been used on small aircraft for reducing torsional stiffness and weight. (CBCPL.)

The hills were long barren in the Copper Basin, as shown in this 1938 photograph. But the people of the area were used to the red hills and the smell of sulfuric acid that they called "the gas." Their fathers, grandfathers, uncles, and husbands had worked for the copper company. Some lived in company houses they had won in the lottery, and they shopped at the company store. Today, many locals speak of these naked hills with a sort of wistful attachment. (LOC.)

8173 F

In the 1920s, the Tennessee Valley Authority (TVA) and state agencies attempted to control erosion of 23,000 acres of land laid bare by fumes from ore roasters using reforestation, which began with the planting of more than eight million trees and the seeding of various grasses. Tennessee

Copper Company also began extensive tree plantings around the same time. In 1941, the TVA started a civilian conservation corps to plant trees in the Copper Basin. (TVA.)

5999F 9-27-38

Largely due to a timber industry boom in the Southeast's mountain states in the early 1900s, Tellico Plains, Tennessee, experienced a significant increase in population. By 1911, Tellico Plains was incorporated, and as many as 2,000 people lived in the community located 36 miles north of Copperhill. Babcock Lumber Company was a large operation in the area. Logging diminished after World War I, and when times became tough, Tellico Plains petitioned the Stokely cannery to come to their town; the company came and employed many residents. In 1938, Copperhill's land was devoid of vegetation, but Tellico Plains, shown here in September of that same year, remained green. (LOC.)

Five

BUMPS IN THE (RAIL)ROAD
BRING NEW CHALLENGES

By the 1930s, rail transportation had improved and opened enough routes that passengers could enjoy meals and overnight berths in comfortable surroundings. The Louisville & Nashville (L&N) Railroad reached its peak in 1931 at 5,266 miles of track. At the same time, the automobile industry had made cars affordable for the middle class, and grand infrastructure, such as bridges, highways, and tunnels, facilitated automobile travel.

Faced with this competition, L&N began appealing to potential passengers by advertising in the *Fannin County Times* newspaper almost monthly as "your hometown friend" who had long been in the area paying taxes and bringing everything necessary for building and furnishing a home.

Eventually, the county, which once had many trains stop on their way through the area, began seeing fewer and fewer engines pause there. L&N weathered the Great Depression by tightening its belt, and it did not suffer as badly as some railroads. By 1940, it still had 4,871 miles of track.

The copper industry moved along as well, and in 1936, Tennessee Copper Company (TCC) purchased Ducktown Chemical and Iron Company, making TCC the sole copper company operating in the Copper Basin until 1987.

The hydroelectric dams built by the Tennessee Valley Authority strove to bring better energy, growth, and economy to Southern Appalachia. The building of Apalachia Dam, with its powerhouse located in Reliance, Tennessee, near the L&N's Old Line, meant electricity for the nearby Polk community. The TVA also taught new farming methods and contributed buildings, such as for schools, to the community.

L&N ended passenger service in Blue Ridge in 1951, but continued it in some areas of its overall railroad into the 1960s. The railroad entered into a few more mergers and marketed itself as Family Lines System for a while before consolidating into the CSX Corporation in 1980. CSX and Norfolk Southern are now the two largest freight railroads in Georgia.

In Manchester, Georgia, 65 miles southwest of Atlanta, Jim Crow laws were still in full effect in 1968. It was the same way north of Atlanta, too, in Cartersville, Blue Ridge, Copperhill, and at other depots. Blacks were supposed to be separated in most everyday environments—at work, school, eating establishments, churches, neighborhoods, and while traveling. The Manchester railroad station (pictured) contained separate waiting rooms and toilets for blacks and whites. Ticket booths were also separate. (LOC.)

In this 1940 photograph, Amy "Sis" Byrd (right) and Charlotte Butler Gordon wait for the train at Curtis Switch, which was a flag stop on the railroad line between Blue Ridge and McCaysville. One only needed to wave or flag down the train at the stop to catch a ride. Curtis Switch got its name from the Richard and Juletta Curtis farmland on which it stood. The stop was four and a half miles southeast of McCaysville. (Steve Byrd.)

Elisha Panter worked at the Tennessee Copper Company during the week and was a photographer on weekends. He worked in the mines for his entire career. This c. 1942 photograph was taken at his home, which was less than a mile behind the TCC plant. Pictured here are, from left to right, (first row) Gertrude Bell Panter (holding Roy Lee Norris Jr.), Marie Panter, Thomas Panter Sr. (holding Thomas Panter Jr.), Bee Hicks, Earl Panter (holding Doris Panter), Barbara Jean Norris, and Elisha Panter (with his arm around Bud Hicks); (second row) Reba Panter, Mae Panter Hicks, Roy Lee Norris, Evelyn Panter Norris (holding Jimmy Norris), Gertrude Ledford Panter (wife of Earl; holding Leland Panter), Ruby Roberts Panter (wife of Thomas), Marie (wife of Claude), and Claude Panter (who was killed in World War II). (Thomas Panter III.)

This group of unidentified railroad executives met in Washington, DC, in the 1930s. During that time, railroads were hit hard by the tough economy. Their competition—the automobile industry—lured more and more consumers away, and the government placed more regulations on railroads. They had to come up with ways to attract business even as they moved from steam-fed to more efficient diesel-fueled engines. When they were granted a freight tariff increase to counter their falling revenues, shippers switched to the less-expensive trucking industry to ship goods. By the middle of 1932, unemployment in the United States had reached an all-time high of 12 million. As the net income of railroads went from a profit of $977 million in 1929 to a loss of $122 million in 1932, railroad employment decreased by 42 percent. (LOC.)

In the pre-1930s South, workers were subject to employers' whims and had no bargaining rights. Then, Pres. Franklin D. Roosevelt's New Deal allowed for unionization. In 1938, the copper miners in the Congress of Industrial Organization (CIO) went on strike for better pay and working conditions. This Marion Post Wolcott photograph shows a group of men sitting near the Ducktown Hotel sign plastered with strike posters. "Scabs" were miners—either regular Tennessee Copper Company workers or new men brought in to replace strikers—who reported to work during the strike. This was a volatile time in the Copper Basin. (LOC.)

In this 1938 photograph, the Tennessee Copper Company train chugs down the tracks in front of the chamber acid plant at Isabella. The black objects at right are acid storage tanks, and the Eureka mine is nearby. (LOC.)

Here, T.A. Aber, the civil engineer who designed the Hiwassee Loop around Bald Mountain, takes the helm of the Hook & Eye local. Aber lived in downtown Atlanta on North Broad Street in the late 1890s but was listed on the 1920 census as rooming with the Coles in Etowah. At that time, he was 63 years old. Norwegian Fred Berg, a 29-year-old machinist in the train shops, was also rooming at the Coles' home. (L&N.)

This image shows the Apalachia Dam (built starting in 1941 and opened in 1943), which operates in Cherokee, North Carolina; underground conduit pipe carries water eight miles to the Georgia border. As early as 1935, the Tennessee Valley Authority recognized that electrical power could provide for great national strength in the event of large-scale war. One reason for building dams was to provide water for Tennessee Valley aluminum production during World War II. The Aluminum Company of America (ALCOA) operated south of Knoxville and became the largest aluminum producer in the world. This photograph shows the lowermost of three dams on the Hiwassee River. The photographer must have been standing above the north end of the railroad relocation and looking down at the river. (TVA.)

Rocky banks above the railroad and below the community of Apalachia Station at the Hiwassee River are indicative of the many rock formations in the area. The fastest and least expensive route for trains involved going around mountains rather than tunneling through them. Obstacles such as these rock bluffs would require much drilling, blasting, and removal of rock, which was being done in the 1940s for dam building. Apalachia Station developed from the need to transport timber and wood chemicals out of the area via train. (TVA.)

McFarland, Tennessee, had a small depot along the tracks. Located approximately 10 miles above Reliance and three miles from the powerhouse, it had a post office, a general store, and a hotel. Residents referred to the train that delivered mail and freight as "The Local." Passenger trains came from Knoxville to Atlanta or from Blue Ridge to Knoxville. (TVA.)

This October 21, 1941, picture shows Jim Allen's homestead, which was removed before the flooding of the Apalachia Dam area. Most people did not complain about losing their land, as they understood the value of the dam for the area. (TVA.)

Apalachia Dam was surveyed for construction on Hiwassee River acreage, the value of which had already been appreciated and appropriated by the Union, Hiwassee-Nolichucky, and Hiwassee River power companies. Since the Tennessee Valley Authority purchased most of the uninhabited land needed for the dam from those companies, they only had to relocate 22 families and 2.5 miles of roads before dam construction could begin. Farner School (pictured) had to be removed, but upon completion of the dam, the TVA left behind one of their construction buildings as a gift to the community for use as a new Farner School. (TVA.)

After Andrew Chadrick's wife died, she left him their children along with those of his deceased sister, so he ordered a bride through the mail. A curious crowd looked on as Knoxville's Myrtle Taylor arrived by train wearing a flower. Chadrick planned on hiding his cane "signal" if he disliked her. They married, but it ended after less than a year; Myrtle left on the same train. This image shows sisters Senia (left) and Minnie Chadrick at the homestead before it was relocated due to construction of the Apalachia Dam. (TVA.)

Men are at work on the roof of the Shearer family's new cabin, which the TVA built after the family was displaced by the construction of the Apalachia Dam. The TVA helped families whose land and homes had to be destroyed for the dam. (TVA.)

19234c

In 1942, TVA photographers recorded laborers grading and Louisville & Nashville Railroad crews laying track for runaround siding—a low-speed section of track—south of Smith Creek. Smith Creek is a feeder stream of the Hiwassee River. The Smith Creek settlement was located between Smith Mountain and the Apalachia powerhouse on the southern side of the Hiwassee. McFarland was upriver from the settlement. (TVA.)

This is a close-up of railroad tracks being laid around the dam area, since track had to be moved in the dam-creating process. The powerhouse is about seven miles from the dam. Train tracks go behind the powerhouse, and penstocks go under the railroad tracks to get to the turbines. A side track went into the powerhouse through a large door. (TVA.)

A surveyor looks at the Apalachia Dam site from above the train tracks during dam construction in 1941. The dam is in a remote, mountainous area that is difficult to access, and the railroad brought in supplies and materials for construction. (TVA.)

In this 1941 image, a Louisville & Nashville Railroad section gang is relocating track to the trestle at the south end of the dam. Trains had been in the area for a long time carrying timber out from logging, transporting passengers, and bringing mail and supplies to the mountain communities. They had been a lifeline for the smaller homestead areas, many of which no longer exist. Now, they were helping to create the dam, which would bring electricity to many and improve living standards. (TVA.)

Section gangs were responsible for the maintenance of a portion of the railway. Crossties had to be changed out, switches lubricated, track components tightened, vegetation (that had grown into the tracks) removed, and ballast—crushed rock—tamped and smoothed because it may have been moved and spread by the weight of the train passing over the tracks repeatedly. Periodic inspections were mandatory. These men, pictured here in 1940, are using a motorized railcar to check their section. (Linda Nickle.)

This c. 1940 photograph shows the last steam freight train out of Copperhill. In the earliest days of the steam engine, James Watt (1736–1819), a Scottish inventor, figured out that steam engines wasted a lot of energy. The cylinder had to be heated and cooled, and Watt developed a separate condenser that made the steam engine more effective and less expensive to use. However, he is better known for a concept he developed that most people utilize every day: the watt. (DBM.)

Concord, Tennessee, rests along the north bank of the Tennessee River, 17 miles west of Knoxville. Concord became a community when the East Tennessee & Georgia Railroad built track there in 1853. This was a large marble shipping area, and several quarries were located nearby. By 1887, Concord had become the second largest town in the state with its business and river trade. The Louisville & Nashville Railroad built the Concord depot in 1902. The Depression, the building of TVA's Fort Loudon Dam, and the growing use of automobiles contributed to the town's isolation and decline. Portions of the railroad had to be removed to higher ground during the dam's construction, and although passenger service was discontinued, some freight continued. Now, with Knoxville's suburban sprawl, Concord's population is again increasing. (McClung-UT.)

The photograph taken near Cleveland shows hopper cars being unloaded via conveyor belt into storage silos. This may be pulpwood being stored for the Bowater paper plant on the outskirts of Cleveland. Bowater, once one of the top landowners in southeastern Tennessee, produced large quantities of newsprint. (CBCPL.)

This 1940s photograph shows a crew of the Louisville & Nashville (L&N) Railroad's Hook and Eye. L&N trains hauled copper, timber, and sulfuric acid over the Hiwassee Loop until 1982, when the line was purchased by Seaboard Systems, which eventually merged with CSX. The loop was used for freight until 2001, after which the Tennessee Overhill Heritage Association purchased it for preservation. The Tennessee Valley Railroad Museum now runs excursions on the loop. (L&N.)

A businessman in a pressed shirt, a tie, and shined shoes dozes while riding in a comfortable passenger car. Across from him, another man also seems quite relaxed with his legs stretched out before him. The last passenger train trip from Copperhill to Knoxville ran in 1951 and was steam-engine driven. At the time, all over the country, railroads were spending large sums of money to trade steam engines for sleek, smooth diesels. (LOC.)

In this late-1930s image, the Blue Ridge Local's train No. 4 leaves Atlanta and heads for Knoxville via the Old Line. As passenger service declined, the railroad incorporated a mail service and the Railway Express freight service for its customers. The Louisville & Nashville Railroad retired its last steam engine from service in 1957. (LOC.)

Blue Ridge Local No. 4—pictured near a quarry in Jasper, Georgia—heads toward Knoxville, which is 213 miles north of Atlanta. Blue Ridge Scenic Railway trainman Larry Dyer states that there was a wooden water tank (for the steam trains) located north of Blue Ridge's Mountain Street. Water was piped down to the tank from a small branch of a stream. (L&N.)

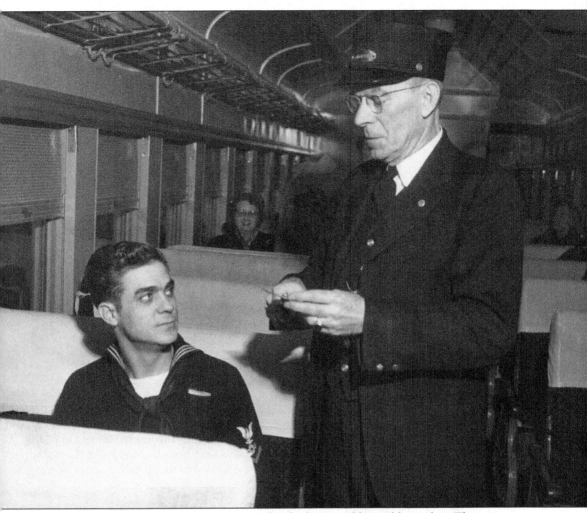

A conductor checks a ticket in this photograph, which is possibly a publicity shot. The passenger train conductor is responsible for safety and operations, and he also sees to passengers' needs. To quote conductor W.T. "Bill" Layton, who retired after 34 years working for the Norfolk & Western Railway: "The conductor runs the train. It's his train from one destination to another." In an interview with Decatur Public Library employee Betty Turnell, Layton also said that conductors handled all bills and reports, attended to cars being removed or added for train configuration, and obeyed all safety rules. Railroading was in Layton's blood, and each trip was exciting no matter how many times he had ridden the route. (L&N.)

In the 1920s and 1930s, trains were equipped with padded seats. This was a change from earlier passenger trains. With a wary eye on the automobile market, railroads shifted more and more toward traveler amenities as an incentive. Passenger trains were first class and had right-of-way over freight passage on the rails. Freight trains had to be cleared to run. (L&N.)

Here is another interior photograph of a passenger train. Some trains had separate seating compartments called roomettes. Passengers traveling in these could lower their seats into beds. Train attendants served meals or snacks. Several businessmen are seated on this train, their luggage tucked into racks above their heads. (L&N.)

Fairmount, a combination depot, was used for both freight and passengers. Crewmen could offload boxcar freight from a side track at the raised platform and transport it directly through the storage area's wide doorway. At the other end of the building, Louisville & Nashville Railroad provided a waiting room for travelers and visitors. In this photograph, the waiting room doorway is visible behind the steel-wheeled Railway Express wagon. (Samuel McMillan Freeman.)

Long before the railroad reached Ball Ground, Georgia, the Cherokee played stickball—a game similar to lacrosse, only rougher—on this land. At the time the town incorporated (around 1883), there were only a few country stores and dwellings in the area. The railroad soon induced population growth by moving quarried marble and other goods out to market and supplies and mail into town. This photograph of the Ball Ground depot is from the 1940s. (L&N.)

Oswald Dome, located in the Cherokee National Forest, sits on the southern side of the Hiwassee River and Old Line tracks three miles west of Reliance, Tennessee. Its elevation is 3,022 feet. Louisville & Nashville Railroad tracks are visible in the foreground in this c. 1950 image. (L&N.)

This is Oswald Dome's original wooden observation tower, which the US Forest Service built around 1920. A later metal tower, which was built around 1930, moved from the mountain to the Ocoee Whitewater Center in 2006. (CBCPL.)

KNOXVILLE, BLUE RIDGE AND ATLANTA

Read Down | Read Up

1 Daily AM	Mls	Table 25 — Eastern Time	4 Daily PM
9.00	0	Lv Knoxville, Tenn. ....Ar	4.50
f...	2	Lv Vestal Lv	
9.09	3	Lv Kingsley Lv	f 4.37
9.13	6	Lv Welwyn Lv	f 4.32
f...	7	Lv Topside } Little River Lv	
9.18	9	Lv Singleton } Lv	f 4.26
f...	11	Lv Chandler Lv	f
9.26	12	Lv Mentor Lv	4.20
9.31	15	Lv Louisville Lv	4.12
9.46	22	Lv Friendsville Lv	3.58
f 9.50	24	Lv Kiser Lv	f 3.53
10.04	30	Lv Greenback Lv	3.39
10.10	31	Lv Jena Lv	3.34
f 10.16	35	Lv McGhee } Little Tennessee River Lv	f 3.26
10.20	38	Lv Vonore } Lv	3.23
f...	41	Lv Kincaid Lv	f
f 10.27	42	Lv Fogin Lv	f 3.16
10.34	46	Lv Madisonville Lv	3.10
10.40	51	Lv Gudger Lv	f 3.03
10.48	56	Lv Englewood Lv	2.55
f 10.56	60	Lv Addison Lv	f 2.48
11.05	64	Ar Etowah Lv	2.41
11.12	64	Lv Etowah ....Ar	2.33
f...	64	Lv Cambria Lv	f
f 11.22	69	Lv Wetmore Lv	f 2.21
f...	71	Lv Austral Lv	f
11.32	75	Lv Reliance Hiwassee River Lv	2.12
f...	76	Lv Probst Lv	f
f 11.37	77	Lv Hiwassee Lv	f 2.07
f...	80	Lv Hood Lv	f..
f...	82	Lv Smith Creek Lv	f
f 11.53	84	Lv McFarland Lv	f 1.52
12.06	90	Lv Apalachia Lv	1.41
12.24	95	Lv Farner Lv	1.24
12.30	98	Lv Turtletown Lv	1.18
f 12.38	101	Lv Horbuck Lv	f 1.10
12.48	106	Lv Ducktown Lv	1.02
1.05	111	Lv Copperhill, Tenn. Ocoee River Lv	12.51
f 1.13	115	Lv Kyle, Ga. Lv	f 12.40
f 1.19	118	Lv Galloway Lv	f 12.33
f 1.22	119	Lv Curtis Lv	f 12.29
1.39	125	Lv Blue Ridge Lv	12.15
f...	128	Lv Maxwell Lv	f
f 1.50	130	Lv Lucius Lv	f 11.59
f 1.54	132	Lv Cherry Log Lv	f 11.55
f 1.59	134	Lv White Path Lv	f 11.49
f...	136	Lv Nicehutt Lv	f...
2.12	140	Lv Ellijay Cartecay River Lv	11.36
f...	144	Lv Ella Gap Lv	f...
f...	146	Lv Tioga Lv	f
f 2.28	147	Lv Totona Lv	11.18
f 2.35	150	Lv Whitestone Lv	11.12
f...	152	Lv Carns Mill Lv	f..
2.45	154	Lv Talking Rock Lv	11.02
3.01	161	Lv Jasper Lv	10.48
3.13	165	Lv Tate Lv	10.36
3.20	168	Lv Nelson Lv	10.26
3.28	172	Lv Ball Ground Lv	10.20
3.34	174	Lv Gober Lv	10.14
3.41	178	Lv Keithsburg } Etowah River Lv	10.06
3.55	183	Lv Canton Lv	9.54
4.02	187	Lv Univeter Lv	9.44
4.07	189	Lv Holly Springs Lv	9.40
4.11	191	Lv Toonigh } Little River Lv	9.36
4.19	195	Lv Woodstock } Lv	9.30
4.29	200	Lv Blackwells Lv	9.18
4.36	203	Lv Westoak Lv	9.11
4.40	205	Lv Elizabeth Lv	9.06
4.45	207	Ar Marietta Lv	9.03
		Chattahoochee River	
5.30 PM	227	Ar Atlanta, Ga. Lv	8.15 AM

MURPHY AND BLUE RIDGE

Read Down | Read Up

109 Ex. Sun. Mixed AM	Mls	Table 26 — Eastern Time	110 Ex. Sun. Mixed PM
10.20	0	Lv Murphy, N. C. ....Ar	3.10
f 10.40	8	Lv Ranger Lv	f 2.32
10.50	11	Lv Culberson, N C Lv	2.25
f 10.57	14	Lv Sweet Gum Ga. Lv	f 2.17
11.15	21	Lv Mineral Bluff Lv	1.55
11.35 AM	25	Ar Blue Ridge, Ga. Lv	1.40 PM

ATHENS AND TELLICO PLAINS

Read Down | Read Up

303 Ex. Sun. Mixed AM	Mls	Table 27 — Eastern Time	304 Mixed AM	302 Mixed AM
8.10	0	Lv Athens, Tenn. ....Ar		7.50
8.40	8	Ar Englewood Lv		7.25
8.40	8	Lv Englewood ....Ar	10.50	AM
f 9.00	10	Ar Nonaburg Lv	10.38	
f 9.20	16	Ar Mt. Vernon Lv	f 10.18	
9.40	23	Ar Tellico Plains, Tenn. Lv	10.01	

McLEANSBORO AND SHAWNEETOWN

Read Down | Read Up

35 Daily Mixed AM	Mls	Table 28	34 Daily Mixed PM
7.15	0	Lv McLeansboro, Ill. ....Ar	12.50
f...	4	Lv Hoodville Lv	f...
7.30	8	Lv Dales Lv	f 11.50
7.55	12	Lv Broughton Lv	f 11.35
8.20	21	Lv Eldorado Lv	11.00
8.30	23	Lv Grayson Lv	f 10.50
f...	24	Lv Brooklyn Lv	f..
8.45	29	Lv Equality Lv	f 10.38
8.55	32	Lv Lawler Lv	f 10.28
9.05	35	Lv Junction Lv	f 10.18
9.35 AM	41	Ar Shawneetown, Ill. Lv	10.00 AM

HARTFORD AND EARLINGTON

Rec ↓ Down | Read Up

31 Ex. Sun. Mixed AM	Mls	Table 29	32 Ex. Sun. Mixed AM
11.20	0	Lv Hartford, Ky. ....Ar	10.55
f...	4	Lv Bishop Lv	f...
f 11.35	6	Lv Centertown Lv	f 10.40
11.55	11	Lv Kronos Lv	10.20
f...	12	Lv Smallhaus Lv	f...
12.15	15	Lv Moorman Lv	10.00
12.30	19	Lv Bremen Lv	f 9.45
f 12.45	21	Lv Lynn City Lv	f 9.30
1.15	23	Lv Millport Lv	9.00
f...	27	Lv Newcool Lv	f...
1.35	30	Lv Anton Lv	f 8.40
2.10	36	Ar Madisonville Lv	8.15
2.20 PM	40	Ar Earlington, Ky. Lv	8.00 AM

EARLINGTON AND CLAY

Read Down | Read Up

40 Ex. Sun. Mixed PM	Mls	Table 30	41 Ex. Sun. Mixed PM
1.35	0	Lv Earlington, Ky. ....Ar	6.10
1.40	4	Lv Madisonville Lv	5.50
f...	11	Lv Manitou Lv	f...
f 2.05	14	Lv Nebo Lv	f 5.15
f...	17	Lv Schmetzers Lv	f...
2.35	21	Lv Providence Lv	4.45
f 3.00	25	Lv Upland Lv	f 3.55
f...	27	Lv Nocturne Lv	f...
3.20 PM	29	Ar Clay Lv	3.30 PM

ELKTON AND GUTHRIE

Read Down | Read Up

23 Tues. Thur. Sat. Mixed AM	Mls	Table 31	24 Tues. Thur. Sat. Mixed AM
7.50	0	Lv Elkton, Ky. ....Ar	7.35
f 7.55	2	Lv Bradshaw Lv	f 7.25
f 8.02	5	Lv Hermon Lv	f 7.18
f 8.10	8	Lv Anderson Lv	f 7.11
8.25 AM	12	Ar Guthrie, Ky. Lv	7.00 AM

REFERENCE NOTES:

C.T.—Central Time
E.T.—Eastern Time.
f Stops on signal.

This 1950 timetable includes scheduled arrivals and departures for both bustling depots and small flag stops along Louisville & Nashville (L&N) Railroad routes, including those between Atlanta and Knoxville. The earliest railroad timetables were short routes posted in newspaper advertisements or printed on broadsides (posters). Eventually, the industry standardized timetables as four inches wide by nine inches tall, and larger railroads had certain covers with their logos or artwork. During World War I, railroads fell under government control for approximately 26 months. Afterward, some railroads—L&N was one—returned to their original timetable formats. L&N's distinctive timetable design remained in place until the end of passenger service in the 1960s. (L&N.)

This gristmill was located just south of Blue Ridge in 1943. According to local historians, it is likely the Ballew mill. Gristmills entered the northern Georgia scene early and were indicators of "good" acreage often noted in sales advertisements as coming "with gristmill." They also often predated a church or school being constructed in a community. (TVA.)

In 1954, a photographer captured this aerial image of the Hiwassee Loop around Bald Mountain. Three states—Tennessee, Georgia, and North Carolina—are visible from the top of the loop. As a train circles the mountain, it will face all four points on a compass. (L&N.)

Tennessee Copper Company produced pig copper in 1901, sulfuric acid in 1907, and built a large-contact sulfuric acid plant in 1942. By 1949, liquid sulfur dioxide was being produced in the new plant. TCC went from making sulfuric acid as a byproduct to becoming a full-fledged chemical plant. Former TCC chemist Richard Jones said of this photograph, "A new general office has just been occupied on the right, a new contact acid plant is in the center, and a new acid office on the left and the beginnings of diversification in the white building where liquid sulfur dioxide will be made. Soon zinc and organic plants will fill out the front range." (CBCPL.)

Railroads helped turn individually owned small-town lumber mills into a burgeoning industry. This June 12, 1951, photograph shows a clinic being held for sawmill owners at a Blue Ridge mill. E.A. Clerenger, of Corley Manufacturing Company in Chattanooga, Tennessee, is shown speaking to the crowd. His company's motto is: "Wood is Wonderful." Corley Manufacturing Company has manufactured and serviced sawmill machinery since 1905. (TVA.)

The 1914–1915 Louisville & Nashville (L&N) Railroad Freight Shipper's Directory, published by the Railroad Advertising Agency, states: "Northern and Eastern capitalists are being attracted to this section by the splendid opportunities the timber land offers. Hundreds of mills are engaged in turning the timber into lumber." The directory referenced Ellijay's Shippen Brothers Lumber Company, which logged over 100,000 acres with one of Georgia's most modern plants on L&N Railroad. This 1951 photograph shows a group of unidentified sponsors and speakers at a sawmill conference. (TVA.)

The *Atlanta Journal* once featured Louis Adams, 97, as Fannin County's oldest citizen. Born in 1862 in Ellijay, notorious hitchhiker Adams did not quit thumbing rides until he was 91. He first worked as a farmhand for room, board, and 25¢; he later sold produce, hauling it either to Benton or Atlanta—he referred to these trips as "going to the railroad." Adams also worked for Tennessee Copper Company. He is pictured here on his daughter Viola Buchanan's Blue Ridge porch. (Janice Rodgers.)

Thomas Panter Jr. sits atop a new Mercury Monterey that his father, Thomas Panter Sr., won on *The Price is Right*. Thomas "Tommy" Panter Sr. worked in the offices at the Tennessee Copper Company. He also holds the record for the most *Price is Right* showcase wins—11 in all. Thomas Panter III said that his grandfather had called places all over the world to figure out prices, taxes, and shipping fees in order to learn the game; he also helped in his community by giving away prizes to those in need. (Thomas Panter III.)

Ralph W. Baugh (pictured), of Mineral Bluff, retired from the Louisville &Nashville Railroad on June 30, 1962, at age 70. By his twenties, he was working as a locomotive fireman in Etowah, Tennessee. Other Baugh family members also worked for the railroad. Ralph's cousin Elsie Baugh was a depot clerk operator by the age of 20 (according to the 1920 census) and was still listed in that occupation in the 1940 census. She married Claude Bryan Higdon, a railroad brakeman, around 1929, and they built a home in Blue Ridge. (FCHF.)

Etowah, with new repair shops, became the headquarters for the Louisville & Nashville (L&N) Railroad's Atlanta Division in 1906. By 1925, over 2,000 employees lived there. Operations declined in the 1930s when steel cars rendered wooden stock repair shops obsolete. Pictured here are, in no particular order, Bill Garwood (engineer), Iky Barone (conductor), Walter Ledford (flagman), John Thomas (baggage), R.W. Baugh (fireman), and Bill Kiser (porter). Inscribed on the back of the photograph, along with the occupants' names, is the accolade "No. 1 in the '30s." (FCHF.)

LOUISVILLE & NASHVILLE
RAILROAD COMPANY

1967-68-69   No. 55410

NOT GOOD on SOUTH WIND, or
GEORGIAN Pullman bet. Chicago and Atlanta-
GEORGIAN Coaches (except bet. St. Louis and Evansville)
CRESCENT and HUMMING BIRD Coaches (except bet.
Nashville, Evansville and St. Louis)

PASS J. F. Cline ----

Pensioned Laborer

L&N RR Co.
OVER ENTIRE SYSTEM
UNTIL DECEMBER 31, 1969, UNLESS OTHERWISE ORDERED WHEN COUNTERSIGNED
BY F. D. BURKE K. W. WISER, R. J. ANDERSON OR J. R. FITZMAYER

This is the railroad employee pass of Frank Cline, a career L&N employee in Etowah, seven miles from his childhood home of Englewood. During World War II, when troop trains passed through, GIs dropped letters in Cline's hat while he serviced trains, and he mailed them to the GIs' homes. In the 1960s, Cline's retirement pension was similar to the benefits offered by Social Security. The National Railroad Retirement System also provides survivor, unemployment, and sickness benefits for career employees. (Dr. David M. Cline.)

Upon his retirement in 1962, Samuel J. Freeman was awarded a gold pocket watch for his 50 years of service to the Louisville & Nashville (L&N) Railroad. These timepieces had certain operating specifications of critical importance in railway transportation. If the engineers' watches were not synchronized, it could spell disaster in the form of a train collision. In fact, time standardization came about in the United States due to the railroads' need for precise timing. Watches were adjusted to keep perfect time in any position. They also included a stabilizing mechanism to protect the timepieces from accidental jarring. There was no stem involved here; first, the crystal was unscrewed and removed, then the lever could be pulled out to set the time. (Samuel McMillan Freeman.)

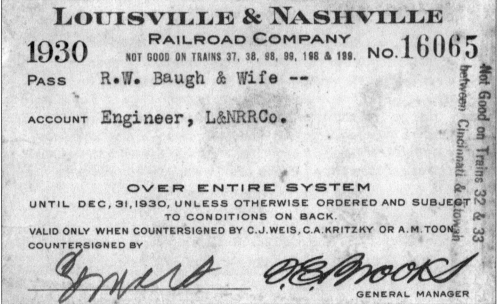

L&N fireman Ralph Baugh, who lived and worked in Etowah in McMinn County, Tennessee, carried this railroad employee pass. L&N issued passes to railroad executives, employees, employees' family members, and special guests. (FCHF.)

Marietta's freight depot no longer exists; it was so badly damaged in a 1970s train derailment that it had to be torn down. The freight depot stood on the other side of the tracks from the passenger depot. Today, a restored Glover Machine Works steam locomotive stands in the freight depot's former location. This is a c. 1950 photograph of the freight depot. (Georgia Department of Natural Resources.)

During the Civil War, Union general William Sherman's fiery march from Atlanta to Macon took him through Marietta, which he set aflame. The town—including the original Western & Atlantic Railroad depot that had instigated the town's incorporation in 1852—was destroyed. The current redbrick station was built in 1898 and has served as the Marietta Welcome Center (located beside the Marietta History Museum) since 1984. The museum is in the Kennesaw House, the hotel where James Andrews and his Union raiders stayed before stealing the train in the Great Locomotive Chase. This photograph is from around 1950. (Georgia Department of Natural Resources.)

James Remley Brumby started the Marietta Barrel Factory in 1867. When flour bags replaced barrels, he switched to making chairs. James and his brother Thomas M. Brumby incorporated the Brumby Chair Company in 1884; James sold his share to Thomas in 1888. This 1950 photograph shows the factory of James's Marietta Chair Company (which eventually competed with Thomas's Brumby Chair Company) alongside the rails. Joel Chandler Harris, presidents, and visitors to resorts across the country have enjoyed chairs made by Marietta's Brumby family—another "manufacturing alongside the railroad" success story. (Georgia Department of Natural Resources.)

James Bolan Glover purchased the Phoenix Foundry, located in Marietta, Georgia, in the early 1890s. With his education in engineering and focus on the needs of various growing industries nearby, he began fashioning equipment that would serve those industries. His company, Glover Machine Works, successfully manufactured many types of steam-powered engines and industrial equipment; his brother John Wilder Glover stepped in upon James's death in 1897 and increased the company's production of steam locomotives. (Georgia Department of Natural Resources.)

Before it closed in 1995, Glover Machine Works created small steam engines for use in the lumber industry, rock quarries, and copper-mine work yards. Glover Machine Works was fully equipped with an iron foundry, machine shop, fabrication and pattern shop, marble polishing machines, quarry cranes, and brick machines. The Southern Museum of Civil War and Locomotive History, located in Kennesaw, houses the Glover Machine Works collection; its unique completeness helped the museum garner its Smithsonian affiliation. (Georgia Department of Natural Resources.)

In 1862, Union troops briefly commandeered Western & Atlantic Railroad's "General" locomotive. Although the 4-4-0 Rodgers, Ketchum & Grosvenor–built steam locomotive was housed in Chattanooga for over 50 years, in 1972, Louisville & Nashville Railroad president William H. Kendall presented the "General" to Georgia through Gov. Jimmy Carter. It is now housed in the Southern Museum of Civil War and Locomotive History in Kennesaw. (CBCPL.)

In May 1960, approximately 50 Louisville & Nashville (L&N) Railroad cars derailed in Eton, Georgia. Derailments occur due to human error, track problems, mechanical issues, signal failures, and weather. Speed can be an issue if brakes are improperly applied. In recent years, derailments have been greatly reduced due to improvements in inspections. One great improvement is the use of ultrasound equipment capable of seeing cracks inside the rails. Here, men use an L&N crane to clean up the site of a train wreck. (CBCPL.)

In this 1965 photograph, a southbound freight train crosses itself on the Hiwassee Loop. Trains on the lower track are only 60 feet below those crossing on the higher trestle. The year 2001 marked the last time a freight train navigated the loop. (L&N.)

The Louisville & Nashville Railroad's Blue Ridge depot is currently in the process of being fully restored. The Blue Ridge City Council recently voted on exterior paint colors—historically accurate gray with white trim—and implemented them with striking effect. The last train came through Blue Ridge on March 23, 1951. (FCHF.)

A lockbox (at far right in the photograph) attached to the outer wall of the Blue Ridge depot was used for freight paperwork left for the depot agent or paperwork he left for the trains. The agent was the operations manager (also called the stationmaster), and he or she oversaw freight and passenger concerns. (FCHF.)

Six

THE RAILROAD'S
MOUNTAIN HERITAGE

Other than the Blue Ridge Scenic Railway, trains no longer travel through Blue Ridge or the Copper Basin, although occasionally Intertrade Holdings, Inc., sells calcine from a copper mine cleanup site to brokers who sell it to foreign buyers and load it into open cars on track along Highway 68.

After the last passenger train departed Blue Ridge in 1951, freight—mostly pulpwood and timber—continued to be shipped through Blue Ridge and Copperhill each week. In 1987, when the Louisville & Nashville (L&N) Railroad ceased operation in the area as a direct result of the end of copper mining (which ceased in the 1980s), L&N sold and leased the track to the Georgia Northeastern Railroad (GNRR), a Class III system purchased in 1990 by private citizen Wilds Pierce. A few years later, the Georgia Department of Transportation (GDOT) bought parts of the line—Whitepath to Blue Ridge, Blue Ridge to McCaysville/Copperhill, and Blue Ridge to Mineral Bluff—and leased the tracks to GNRR.

Reforestation began before the 1930s and continued over the decades. Today, Glenn Springs Holdings employees work with the Environmental Protection Agency and Tennessee Department of Environment and Conservation (TDEC) to continue the cleanup of pollutants. While locals recall the bare, dusty mounds that surrounded them in earlier decades, visitors to the area now see only grassy, forested hills.

The railroad had come to the Blue Ridge area for the copper mines and gradually disappeared once the mines were gone. In the late 1990s, a group of Blue Ridge citizens met and began brainstorming a plan to bring the train back. Thanks to their hard work, today's visitors can ride the Blue Ridge Scenic Railway and learn about the area's rich history and beauty. The region remains much as it was in 1876, when Col. R.F. Maddox sent a description of his trip to the area to the *Atlanta Constitution*:

"It is different than any other portion of the state. There are no tables or uplands. It is all mountains and valleys. The latter are very rich and productive. The mountains are high and so steep that no portion of them can be cultivated, but the variety of minerals which lie abundantly in and beneath them make them far more valuable than any soil on earth. Along the entire line the country is a most beautiful one, the scenery is grandly picturesque and for beauty cannot be surpassed . . . all along the line magnificent water powers, the streams are many, and are as clear as crystal, rushing from every mountain."

Postelle, Tennessee, first known as Ducktown Station, was once a town with a train depot made from a boxcar. The Louisville & Nashville (L&N) Railroad built a new depot there in 1913, and L&N employees built homes in the town, along with a store, a church, and a school. Both depots are now gone, and the tracks are vacant. (Author's collection.)

Postelle Road travelers are greeted by this welcome sign in front of a church. Incorporated in 1899 upon the arrival of Knoxville Southern Railroad, the town was named in honor of Dr. Joseph M. Postelle (1865–1939), an Indiana-born physician who practiced in the area. (Author's collection.)

The Hiwassee Loop was saved from demolition by the Tennessee Overhill Association in partnership with Glenn Springs Holdings, the subsidiary of Oxy Petroleum that was cleaning the old Tennessee Copper Company mining property. The Tennessee Overhill Association purchased the line in 2002, and they run a 3.5-hour sightseeing excursion much like that of the Blue Ridge Scenic Railway. The loop's tracks are high atop wooden trestles; if a train is more than 80 cars long, it will reach a point where it catches up to itself. (Ron Henry Collection.)

Mineral Bluff Depot, which is listed in the National Register of Historic Places, was built from locally made brick and is the only Western & Atlantic depot still standing. Each month, the Tri-State Model Railroaders meet here to work on a visitor-friendly HO scale Hook and Eye Division model train layout. (Author's collection.)

The Western & Atlantic Railroad built this depot in Cartersville, approximately 40 miles north of Atlanta, in 1854. It survived the Civil War, but there is a bullet hole in its outer brick wall. It has been restored, but a brick wall saved from the older version of the depot shows some beautiful original frieze work. The depot is much smaller than it once was, as its long freight warehouse was demolished in 1972. (Author's collection.)

Since 2001, Glenn Springs Holdings Company's group of 99 employees at Copperhill has been working to restore the property for Occidental Petroleum. According to Glenn Springs Holdings Company, it is the largest reclamation project in the Southeast. In this 1960 image, a photographer has captured an unidentified man gazing at the Tennessee Copper Company plant. (CBCPL.)

Open cars sit alongside the tracks across from the former Tennessee Copper Company (TCC) plant, which now houses Glenn Springs Holdings Company. TCC's Burra Burra Mine closed in 1959. Cities Services Company purchased TCC in 1963 and continued to produce acid and other chemicals for decades at the company site. Acid production ended in 2000, and cleanup began in 2001. From time to time, these cars are filled with iron calcine, which foreign buyers process into steel. Slag is another byproduct of the mining; the nonmetallic dust, soot, and rock can be recycled into a product used in the building industry for sandblasting or cleaning equipment and furnaces. It can also be mixed with paint or concrete as a binding agent. (Author's collection.)

Pictured here are the first conductors of the Blue Ridge Scenic Railway, Ray Leader (left) and Del Kittendorf. The Blue Ridge Scenic Railway opened for business in May 1998, blowing the customary "all aboard!" in Blue Ridge before carrying passengers on an easy 13-mile ride along the Toccoa River to McCaysville. When it is time to return, the train, which has engines on both ends, simply heads back to Blue Ridge without even having to turn around. (Edye Daetwyler.)

Carl Hymen helped clear track of rotten crossties, damaged rails, and brush between Ellijay, Blue Ridge, and McCaysville before the Blue Ridge Scenic Railway began its journey in 1998. This laborious work was slowly accomplished with motorized railcars that could travel the damaged tracks. Railcar owners worked together to clear various spots. Hymen, the first engineer of the Scenic, is a longtime collector of antique railroad motorcars and a member of the North American Railcars Operators Association (NARCOA), a group of 1,800 worldwide members dedicated to the upkeep and safe and legal use of historical rail equipment. (Edye Daetwyler.)

This photograph shows some of the BRSR volunteer crew members in front of a converted boxcar acquired from the Great Smoky Mountain Railroad and originally named "The Alarka Creek" (after a waterway along its previous route) but now referred to as No. 697. Pictured here are, from left to right, (first row) Jerry Coile, unidentified, Larry Dyer, Paul Lanager, Ray Leader, and unidentified; (second row) Bill Purdy, David Alden, Randy Minter, Jim Minter, Greg Weaver, unidentified, Brian Anglin, Bill Clewell, John Wilding, and Dick Hillman; (third row, inside boxcar) unidentified, Judy Johnson, Carolyn Wilding, Dave Lathrop, Kim Raburn, Diane Kittendorf, Del Kittendorf, unidentified, and unidentified. (BRSR.)

This sleek Blue Ridge Scenic Railway car is resting on its track on an overcast day. While riding the train, one can pass through its interesting variety of cars with seating ranging from cushioned individual seats to benches in enclosed or open cars. The Scenic also includes a concession car, a restroom, a gift shop, and a handicapped car with a wheelchair lift. The Scenic began with five cars in 1998 and now has ten passenger cars, one commissary, and two engines. (BRSR.)

The Scenic is filled with passengers in this 2011 photograph. In 2013, around 70,000 people took the trip on the Scenic. During the first year (1998), the railway hosted more than 17,000 day-trippers. On a recent run, various participants, when asked why they were riding that morning, replied: "it's a 50th anniversary trip," "I've never ridden a train before," "I'm giving my grandson an experience lots of people will never have again," and "it was on my bucket list." (BRSR.)

The Scenic is a Louisville & Nashville Heritage Railroad. These trains are usually formed from historic engines and cars retired from commercial railroads. Heritage trains employ volunteers, who are often railfans. These volunteers help to assist riders with climbing aboard and disembarking, and they also note the trip's scenery. (BRSR.)

The Blue Ridge Scenic Railway takes a smooth path through the woods and along the Toccoa River past farms, churches, and homes. The train has two engines—one on each end, so the train can return along the same route without reversing—and 11 cars. (BRSR.)

The Scenic's course passes three ghostly former rail stops. Curtis Switch was the scene of a bad train wreck in 1928, when depot agents could not warn northbound and southbound engineers in time to divert one of their two trains. The head-on collision killed one engineer and badly injured his son, who was the fireman. Kyle, a whistle stop that offered mail service, and Galloway, a regular stop with a post office, are now overgrown mountainsides. (BRSR.)

The Scenic crosses the Toccoa River on the nearly-300-foot-long Toccoa River Bridge, a Baltimore riveted truss bridge built by the Louisville & Nashville Railroad in 1926. Baltimore trusses have a simple and strong design, with extra bracing in the lower truss, well suited for railroads. The bridge passed to CSX but is now owned by the Georgia Northeastern Railroad. As the train prepares for crossing, passengers are warned to keep their hands inside, as it is an excitingly tight pass over this bridge. (BRSR.)

This is the Blue Ridge Scenic Railway diesel engine. Diesels run cleaner and far more efficiently than steam engines. The first engines on the Scenic were engines No. 2097 and No. 4125. The train currently runs from March through December and is especially popular during the fall in the Chattahoochee-Oconee National Forests. (BRSR.)

Carl Hymen, who has worked with the Blue Ridge Scenic Railway from its beginning, was helping with the North American Railcar Operators Association on this particular Saturday; the group had just taken an outing on the Scenic's rails. (Author's collection.)

Blue Ridge Scenic Railway passengers disembark in McCaysville after the first half of the trip. They have time for a leisurely lunch and exploration of the historic side-by-side towns of McCaysville, Georgia, and Copperhill, Tennessee. One can straddle the blue line in the IGA Hometown Foods parking lot and be standing in two states at once. (BRSR.)

Over 150 years ago, the Cherokee created fish traps—large, V-shaped stone formations—in the Toccoa River between Blue Ridge and McCaysville. Men would usher the fish toward the wide mouth of the V, and when the fish became trapped at its point, women and children would scoop them up. The waters of the Toccoa run fast and shallow and are very clear; this photograph shows the river as viewed from the Scenic. (Author's collection.)

BIBLIOGRAPHY

Barclay, R.E. *The Railroad Comes to Ducktown*. Waynesville, NC: Don Mills Inc., 1996.

Brands, H.W. *American Colossus: The Triumph of Capitalism, 1865–1900*. New York: Knopf Doubleday Publishing Group, 2010.

Buehler, Ingrid and Caldwell, Linda. *The Old Line Railroad*. Etowah, TN: Polk County Publishing, 2009.

Cain, Hugh. "The L&N's 'Old Line': The Hook & Eye Division." *Dixie Line*. (June 1998): 4-6.

George, Michael. *Louisville and Nashville's Atlanta Division*. Collegedale, TN: The College Press, 2000.

glennsprings-copperbasinproject.com

Hallberg, M.C. *Railroads in North America*. 2009.

A History of Tennessee. Nashville, TN: The Goodspeed Publishing Company, 1887.

Industrial and Freight Shippers Directory of Louisville and Nashville Railroad. Louisville, KY: University of Louisville Archives and Records Center, 1914–1915.

Laney, F.B. and Emmons, W.H., with the active collaboration of Arthur Keith. "Geology and Ore Deposits of the Ducktown Mining District, Tennessee." Washington, DC: Department of the Interior, Washington Printing Office, 1926.

Lillard, Roy G. *The History of Bradley County*. Cleveland, TN: East Tennessee Historical Society, 1976.

Marlin, Rev. Lloyd G. *The History of Cherokee County*. Atlanta, GA: Walter W. Brown Publishing Company, 1933.

McAfee, Broadus. "The 'Old L&N' and the 'New L&N' Railroad Lines Sometimes Called the 'Hook and Eye' and the 'Low Line': A Bit About Northwest Georgia Along the Way." *Northeast Georgia Historical Genealogical Society*, 1979.

McAllister, Tracy. *Georgia Comprising Sketches of Counties, Towns, Events, Institutions, and Persons, Vol. II*. 1906.

Rush, Ken. "The Copper Basin Story." Presentation, Ducktown Basin Museum. Ducktown, GA: 2009.

Snell, William R. *Cleveland the Beautiful*. Nashville, TN: Williams Printing Company, 1986.

Solomon, Brian and Cooper, Bruce C. *The Classic Eastern American Railroad Routes*. New York: Chartwell Books Inc., 2011.

tennesseeoverhill.com/heritage/old-line-railroad/

Thompson, Kathy. *Blue Ridge Historic Home & Towns, Blue Ridge Lake, The Cohutta Wilderness, Railroad History, and More*. Blue Ridge, GA: Thompson Publishing, 2011.

Ward, George G. *The Annals of Upper Georgia Centered in Gilmer County*. Nashville, TN: The Parthenon Press, 1994.

Visit us at
arcadiapublishing.com

···

CPSIA information can be obtained
at www.ICGtesting.com
Printed in the USA
LVOW03*1244091016

508020LV00015B/153/P